ADVANCED BRAZILIAN JIU-JITSU TECHNIQUES

MARCELO GARCIA

with Marshal D. Carper & Glen Cordoza

LAS VEGAS

First Published in 2011 by Victory Belt Publishing.

ISBN 13: 978-1-936608-82-9

This book is for educational purposes. The publisher and authors of this instructional book are not responsible in any manner whatsoever for any adverse effects arising directly or indirectly as a result of the information provided in this book. If not practiced safely and with caution, martial arts can be dangerous to you and to others. It is important to consult with a professional martial arts instructor before beginning training. It is also very important to consult with a physician prior to training due to the intense and strenuous nature of the techniques in this book.

Cover Design by Jimmy Smith

Technique Photography by Glen Cordoza

Printed in The USA

CONTENTS

2. ESTABLISHING BACK CONTROL

BACK BODY LOCK

SECURING THE SECOND HOOK

COUNTER TACTICS

3. SUBMISSIONS FROM BACK CONTROL

4. TAKEDOWNS

5. ATTACKING THE GUARD

BREAKING THE CLOSED GUARD

PASSING THE OPEN GUARD

PASSING THE HALF GUARD

PASSING THE BUTTERFLY GUARD

6. SUBMISSIONS

CHOKES

ARMBARS AND OMOPLATAS

COUNTER OMOPLATA DEFENSE

ACKNOWLEDGMENTS

This book couldn't have been done without the support and help of so many people, but first I want to thank my family for always being there for me since the beginning:

To my father: Marcio Vespucio and in memory of my mother Luzia Garcia.

My sister, Monica; my brother in law, Gerson; and my brother, Pedro.

My beautiful wife, Tatiana Tognini Garcia, and my dear friend Josh Waitzkin, you helped me make my dreams come true!

To all my teachers, Iran Brasileiro, Paulo Rezende, and Fabio Gurgel.

A special thanks to the mginaction crew,
who worked so hard to put this book together!

Katya Waitzkin
Jimmy Smith
Emily Kwok
Jordan Blevins

To my friends and teachers at my school

Henrique Rezende
Paul Schreiner

To all my students, you are all a part of this story!

Photography credits

Thanks to all the photographers
that contributed to this book:

Alicia Anthony - AliciaPhotos.com
John Ricard / www.johnricard.com
John Lamonica - F575@Mac.com

My friend Mark Bocek training in NY.

Worlds 2010.

My 2010 quarter finals.

Worlds 2011, my 5th world title as a black belt at middleweight.

My 2010 quarter finals.

My dear wife Tati and great friend and supporter Liborio at the MGInAction booth at Worlds 2011.

Pic taken during my final match in 2011 — Fabio Gurgel, Henrique, Tati, and some of my students.

INTRODUCTION

by Josh Waitzkin

The Long Beach Pyramid is rocking with Brazilian chants and stomps, bleachers shaking, tension wild and thick. The middleweight final of the 2010 Mundials has come down to its last eight seconds. Marcelo Garcia and Claudio Calasans are 9:52 into an all-out war. The action is stopped and the fighters will reset in the middle of the ring. Marcelo is up 2 points. His road to this moment has been treacherous. Here is a man who thrives in fast-paced, dynamic, transitional flow, but who has navigated a stacked bracket of closed guards and tight grips, opponents doing everything they can to lock him down and keep him away from his game.

Marcelo's friends and coach scream for him to back up once the clock starts. Just don't engage. You are seconds from winning the world championship, man. "Just back up, Marcelinho!" Everyone is saying the same thing, but I know there isn't a chance. Marcelo doesn't know how to fight backing up. This is a man who moves forward.

Marcelo on "Go!" in the final 8 seconds against Claudio Calasans at the 2010 World Championships

The ref says "Go," and Marcelo stands like a matador. Calasans is a world-class wrestler and judoka on top of his incredible jiu-jitsu. Takedowns are his bread and butter. He immediately shoots hard for a double, Marcelo sprawls, and Calasans scoots deep under for a butterfly sweep going right, then left, then right again. Marcelo surfs on top of it and like lightning Claudio jumps up for an uchimata, a textbook judo throw, pulling at the elbow of Marcelo's base hand, getting nowhere, and then he dives back under for the most dangerous butterfly sweep yet.

2010 World Champ

Uchimata

Marcelo backsteps, his right leg reposting in a blur, riding all this like a wave. I've never seen so much happen in eight seconds in my life. Time expires in the frenzy. Marcelo, reaches down and pulls Claudio to his feet, they hug, two warriors who in that moment understand one another better than anyone on the planet. Garcia has won the world championship again. He'd later tell me those last eight seconds were his favorite of the tournament. Good to know—he almost gave his wife and friends heart attacks. From a competitive perspective, it was madness for him to take that risk. I can hardly imagine another competitor who would have done it. But then again, I've never known someone who loves what he does so purely.

An hour later, Marcelo, his devoted, soulful wife Tati (also a BJJ black belt), and a busload of students and friends are leaving the Pyramid to go to a celebration dinner. Marcelo is driving, and as he pulls onto the street something catches his eye. He brakes, turns the van around. Everyone is hungry, celebrating, riding high from the adrenaline of the tournament. Marcelo drives back to the far end of the emptying parking lot, where an Italian couple is bent down staring at their car hood. The rental is crippled, it won't start, and they don't know what to do. Marcelo met the couple briefly at the tournament. They shook hands once. Now he gets out and asks them if he can help. Tati does the same. The couple can't believe that Marcelo Garcia is asking about their car minutes after he won the world championship. Tati calls the rental company, Marcelo chats, relaxed, easy, not a hint of rush, tells them everything will be fine. There is something so humble about this moment, so human. He is a world away from all the glory. Tati puts everything in order for the Italians, arranges for a car to come for them. Marcelo shakes hands with the couple and we drive off.

I've seen many world championships won and lost—if there is ever a time for narcissism, this is it. Not Marcelo. As his friend, business partner, and student, that scene in the parking lot meant more to me than anything I've seen him do on the mats.

Since this is a book about Marcelo Garcia's technical repertoire, I thought the most helpful way to structure the introduction would be to give readers an inside perspective on the thematic architecture that runs beneath. Countless grapplers try to replicate what Marcelo does on the mats without understanding the operating principles of his personality and learning process—perhaps this will help fill in some of the foundation.

If you were to frame Marcelo's mind and life through four themes, you could go a long way toward understanding most of his decisions. First, the love. He lives true to himself. Second, kinesthetics—he cultivates and is guided by a remarkable physical intelligence. Third, he is a relentless learning machine—his whole training style is designed for nonstop growth, and he rarely if ever repeats errors (which is a rather unique trait). Fourth, an unwillingness to back down from a challenge. If you tell him he can't do something, for better or worse, he will prove you wrong.

Looking at where Marcelo is in his life today makes a lot of sense through that lens. He lives in New York City because he *feels* better here than anywhere else. His school, located in the heart of Manhattan, is an Open Academy. Anyone is welcome to come train, regardless of affiliation. Marcelo has no time for politics. If you love grappling, you are invited. He will greet you with a big smile and a handshake and he will train with you. Because he loves training. He is up to the challenge. And he will probably learn more than you from the exchange.

The Love

If I had to describe Marcelo Garcia in a few words they would be all about the love. He lives in tune with his essence. He surrounds himself with people, food, and places that make him feel good about life. He trains *hard* twice a day five times a week because there is nothing he would rather do.

But it goes deeper than this. Marcelo *needs* the love. And he cultivates it with his style of training (movement), with his food (he will journey for it), his crazy frogger-style fixed gear biking through NYC (*perhaps too much movement*).

Marcelo in the city he loves, unfortunately without a helmet. Please send him an e-mail at marcelo@mginaction.com and encourage him to wear one!

If I think back to one of the most difficult stages of his life, when he was living in Florida and training MMA, contractually prohibited from competing in BJJ tournaments, preparing for MMA fights but then having them pulled away from him by promoters at the very end of training camp, again and again—I realize it was Marcelo's kryptonite. Since he was a boy he has trained and competed—for Marcelo these are intertwined and nourishing—now for reasons he did not understand, he could not do what he had always loved.

He went up to 202 pounds (Marcelo usually walks around at 180). He didn't smile as much. He looked older, less joyful. I think he learned a lot about how he wants to live from that frustrating period.

The Feeling

Marcelo is as kinesthetically intelligent as you get. His internal compass is feeling. If he meets someone and we are discussing him later, Marcelo will tell me about how the guy makes him feel. "I feel good around him" or "I don't know, Josh," with a slight shake of the head (this is Marcelo, about the nicest guy on the planet, not feeling good about someone). When we were searching for spaces for our NYC school, he would know whether he liked the place or not by whether he felt good in there. I was looking at dimensions, mat space, potential wind circulation, plumbing for showers, office area, over a hundred locations, variables flying through my head—a chess player's burden—"I feel good here, Josh." We had our school.

It's also important to understand how kinesthetic intelligence moves Marcelo on the mats. It is not so widely known, but Marcelo does not study his opponents. When I first realized this, given my background as a professional chess player (chess players study the repertoires of their opponents as precisely as possible), I thought it was insane. But as I have gotten to know Marcelo more deeply over the years, and as we have discussed this in detail, I have learned why it works for him so well.

Think about this through the lens of MGInAction, our online training program that essentially opens up Marcelo's game to as scientific and thorough an investigation as the user wants. When I first proposed MGInAction to Marcelo, the primary concern of mine was whether it would be disastrous for an active competitor, let alone the very best in his field, to open his laboratory to all his rivals. On the program, users (and opponents) can watch Marcelo teach all of his techniques; they can watch his training every day from his school; they can use the sophistication of Marcelo's database to search for his weaknesses. We hold nothing back. There are no secrets. Can you imagine an NFL or NBA team doing such a thing all season long, let alone in the weeks before the playoffs? Marcelo's perspective on this is profoundly refreshing—"If someone studies my game they will be entering my game. And I know it better than they ever will." Simple as that. So far he has been proven right.

This is why Marcelo doesn't study his opponents. Because then he feels he will be entering *their* games. Ideally, Marcelo will watch one match of an opponent. "I want to see how they start the match so I'm not surprised. I want to impose my game and I think I can impose my game from many places. But I want to see if they do something crazy. Will I have time to get my grips before pulling guard? Are they going to shoot right away? Or will they wait a little, pace themselves, and then I'm gonna go for a takedown. I just watch to see what might surprise me before I impose my game."

In reading this, it's important to keep in mind the other side of the equation: while Marcelo doesn't do a deep study of opponents beforehand, he picks up on their patterns while rolling with them at a speed that is stunning. You'll be amazed if you watch his competition and training footage with this in mind. I've made a lifelong study of this theme, and Marcelo unearths and exploits tells faster than any mental or physical competitor I've seen. To take it one step further, it is hard for me to recall ever seeing someone catch Marcelo twice with the same takedown, sweep, or pass, let alone submission. Given Marcelo's lifestyle of nonstop training with the best in the world, that is an incredible statement.

Learning

Marcelo's repertoire is in a constant state of evolution, and experimentation is a key part of his process—he is often playing with things around the edges of his arsenal, testing, pushing his boundaries. This is part of how his game always tends to be one step ahead of his opponents. I recall one period a few years ago when he was experimenting with a certain kind of pressure from the mount. He was tapping tough and strong brown and black belts from abdominal pressure alone—he'd get you breathing hard and then fill the space when you exhaled. Problem is you couldn't get that space back so after a while you couldn't breathe and were using two hands to fight off his hips, begging him to choke you so there would be an honorable way out. This mount was the most

incredible pressure I've felt in BJJ. But then one day he dropped it. Not for him.

Similarly, one day on the mats, after years of my pestering him about the D'arce (it had been a favorite submission of mine—Marcelo will not use it because it is "strength-based"), Marcelo decided to teach me a lesson and submitted me twice with it in one roll. Strongest D'arce I ever felt, by far. He never used it again—"I had to squeeze too hard, Josh." Honestly, in this case I think I took one for the team—the rest of you won't have to deal with it. I have the impression that if someone went around collecting all the techniques that *almost* made it into Marcelo's repertoire, they would have quite an arsenal—but it would be helpful to discuss a core axiom of how he decides what stays or goes.

When studying Marcelo's technical repertoire, it's absolutely critical to understand a core principle of his training philosophy: he only uses techniques that will work against opponents who are bigger and stronger than him. Marcelo grew up competing in absolute divisions since he was a blue belt, so the origin of this approach is no mystery. It's also highly efficient—if something feels like it takes too much strength, Marcelo rejects it. This is why you will never (unless he is training a student's

One of Marcelo's favorite submissions, the North South Choke.

awareness) see Marcelo use head and arm chokes or kimuras, for example. He does not believe they will work against someone much stronger. His North South choke, on the other hand, isolates the neck and will work against a gorilla.

Another key principle of Marcelo's learning style is movement. His top pressure is devastating when he wants it to be, but in training Marcelo rarely stops moving. He does not hold you down but lets you move and expose yourself. This makes his mat time highly efficient, as he is maximizing the amount of time spent in transition. He also never rests in a bad position. Whenever you feel like you are passing Marcelo's guard, he has a way of bouncing you away like a giant balloon. He never lets you settle in a good position, and he is a master of all the transitional windows that precede a dominant position. Put these together, and he's an awfully tough guy to pin down.

One of many manifestations of the balloon effect (anyone who trains with Marcelo knows it well).

There is another learning tool of Marcelo's that might be helpful. Marcelo mirrors brilliantly. A few examples—we were on my boat, fishing, diving, and paddleboarding for a week in the Bahamas. It was interesting to observe him as a total beginner—the fastest water learner I've ever seen. In one revealing moment, I was showing him how to handle the lines and use the outriggers. I showed him the correct way, then I showed him how not to do it so he would understand a common mistake. "Don't show me that, Josh," he said. "Just show me the right way." He does not learn intellectually, with dos and don'ts—he learns by seeing and doing things with quality. Similarly, he once told me about the time that he was skateboarding and he nearly broke his ankle going down a ramp. He had done four or five great runs before the last fall. He was seriously injured, but he made himself get back on and do one more good run so that was what was left in his mind before he stopped. If he ended doing it right, right would stick.

A jiu-jitsu manifestation of his mirroring: If you are in the school a lot, and you know him well enough, every once in a while you'll notice Marcelo playing in a certain style to train his students to deal with techniques that are completely outside of his repertoire— for example the 50/50 or various inverted sweeps. *Without a single practice rep*, Marcelo enters and plays these guards like a virtuoso—because he has watched and felt them when they've been played against him, and he just internalized the right way to do it. He has never "studied" or "drilled" these guards. It's more like he has soaked them in by visual and kinesthetic osmosis. After the session you wonder how good he would be if he used these techniques too, but he dismisses the idea altogether (they don't *feel* right for him and they won't work against much larger opponents). To really understand Marcelo's

In the zone at the 2010 Mundials Final.

mind, and how he learns, I think one needs to dwell on the unobstructed relationship between his visual and kinesthetic processing. Perhaps his relative lack of abstract conceptual thinking is helpful to him in this regard.

One final theme I'd like to discuss is presence. Concentration is a key component of Marcelo's day-to-day and competitive life, and I think it is a big reason why he can learn and perform so efficiently. When he shakes hands with you, he is concentrating on you. When he rolls with you, you are his universe. When he eats food, he really focuses on and enjoys that food. When he laughs, he laughs with his whole being. The abilities to turn it on and turn it off are both key strengths that Marcelo cultivates in little moments and utilizes under pressure.

Along these lines, watching Marcelo closely at World Championships you are struck by both his unparalleled intensity on the mats and his tremendous relaxation between fights. When he is fighting he is lit up with a laser focus that is impenetrable . . . and between matches his face and manner are soft like a teddy bear. In this year's 2011 Mundials, Marcelo was sleeping literally five minutes before his semifinal.

Usually he sleeps until he is about fifteen minutes from a match. He does a mellow stretching routine, doesn't watch the action on the mats. He'll actually turn his back to the action if the crowd erupts and he is tempted to look. Fans who ask for a picture or an autograph will not run into a fighter bursting with pre-battle tension, but a warm handshake and a patient smile. Marcelo yawns while he walks to the ring. Then he steps in, slaps hands, and turns it on all the way. Sports psychologists have done studies on the importance of releasing the mind before intense engagement. NFL quarterbacks are observing that they play better if they don't watch their defense on the field. Tennis players and golfers build routines to help themselves turn it off between shots or points. There is a science behind this. But no one taught this science to Marcelo.

He grew up competing in absolute divisions (from blue belt on) usually having around nine fights in a day, sometimes with a two-hour break between his weight division and the absolute. He would watch the fights while waiting, and he would get emotionally drained. Then one time he accidentally fell asleep while waiting. He didn't hear the organizers calling for him and his friend woke him up in a panic. Marcelo ran to the ring, wiped the sleep from his eyes, and fought beautifully. He won the tournament and learned an important lesson. Then, years later, in his first black belt world championship he was watching the early fights and his heart started racing. "I was sitting to compete, and my heart was beating so fast. I thought I gotta control this. I made myself calm. Now I try to get the most calm possible. The calmer I feel, the better I will do in the fight." So he sleeps.

The Challenge

Marcelo first came to the United States in 2006 and his lifestyle involved a lot of travel and seminars. Twice a month he would fly to a grappling or MMA school, usually in the United States, and teach a two-day seminar. Each day of the seminar was structured with a brief warm-up, technique work for about an hour, and then forty to sixty minutes of sparring. During this sparring phase all the toughest bruisers at the school would line up and go after Marcelo.

Marcelo sleeping minutes before the finals of the 2011 World Championships.

I've seen it many times. Sometimes the energy is good, but sometimes you have well-rested 240-pound beasts trying to tear him apart, one after the next.

I've never seen or heard of another martial artist exposing himself in that way during regular seminars. Of course part of it can be explained by Marcelo's supreme confidence. Another element is the fact that this was a great learning opportunity for him—consistent exposure to different repertoires and a whole lot of heat. Marcelo also felt that people came to see and feel him in action, and it was his responsibility to comply.

In my opinion, however, the largest element is that Marcelo loves a challenge . . . and again, this is in both little moments and big. During warm-ups at our school, Marcelo always calls over the most athletic young bull to race against him in the crab walk or some other physical test. If someone casually mentions that he probably can't jump from one place to another, hold your breath because he's gonna fly.

I saw this most literally one evening in the Bahamas when my dad asked Marcelo if he thought he could jump from the stern of our boat to the dock which was seven or eight feet away and two feet above the gunnel. The second I heard the question I knew what was coming. Marcelo looked over the expanse of water crisscrossed with dock lines that could easily trip him up—if he came up short he'd smash his shin, crack his head, and plunge into the harbor with the sharks we'd just been feeding. My dad realized he was really going to try and said "No Marcelo! I was kidding. Please don't!" Marcelo quietly walked inside

Marcelo embracing his wife and loving companion, Tati, after he wins the finals at the 2011 Mundials—His 5th Black Belt World Championship title.

Marcelo leaping over Big Chris during warm ups in late 2009, while the NYC Academy was still under construction.

the boat and we breathed a sigh of relief. He slipped his iPhone out of his pocket, walked out, and got back up on the gunnel. Before we knew it, his right leg swung like a pendulum and he launched off his left. Well, it was a close shave. He ended up reaching the dock with his right big toe and pulling himself up with it like an orangutan (oh yes—Marcelo's toes work like fingers). Then he turned to us with that world-class smile that said in the sweetest way, don't challenge me, guys, or you're gonna lose.

I find that brilliant people's weaknesses are often hidden in the folds of their strengths, and Marcelo is no exception. For example, Marcelo's love for the beauty of transitional, fast paced jiu-jitsu surely takes away from the time he might spend practicing inside the closed guard. One could make the argument that Marcelo's dismissal of "size- or strength-based techniques" have left him relatively vulnerable to triangles, a kimura, and a D'arce over the years. If you look at the very end of the 2009 ADCC Finals and the last eight seconds of the 2010 Mundials that I described above, you could surely see a potential weakness born

of idealism—a purist's inability to buck a challenge, the need to show a rival that he doesn't have to hold on to win, even for a second. Will opponents learn from this and try to push Marcelo's buttons to make him react to the challenge instead of imposing his game? Will they try to piss him off to get in the way of his relaxation? Will they keep him away from the jiu-jitsu that he loves, stalling even when they are down on points (the ultimate compliment, perhaps), hoping that he will be the one to take risks even when he is winning? Probably. But he's a pretty fast study and he's on to them. I'd bet on Marcelo.

Josh Waitzkin,
author, The *Art of Learning*

New York City. August, 2011

As you study the techniques in this book

you'll find that we've inserted MGInAction 'Helpful Hints' and Marcelo Garcia 'Fast Facts'. The hints are filled with useful information on how to best utilize MGInAction.com, and the facts present some interesting details about Marcelo's game.

MG FAST FACT

HELPFUL HINT

Our Virtual Academy and Grappling Database features thousands of videos with new content uploaded on a daily basis. At MGInAction.com you have the option to watch **Sparring sessions, Instructionals** (videos in which Marcelo instructs and demonstrates the technique) or **InAction clips** (quick 'real time' highlights of Marcelo performing a technique in sparring). MgInAction.com aims to teach you through both theory and practice, and our website interface has many unique tools to help you with this. We've created a **User Guide** (you can find it after this article) to point out some of the tools that are at your disposal. If you are not a member on MGInAction.com, you can take this opportunity to look at our customizable interface. For those who are members, check to see if you're getting the maximum benefits.

The team at MGInAction.com constantly strives to improve and expand our site so that our members can take their study to the next level. We not only update content, but we're constantly adding creative tools for your benefit to our interface (like the new mirroring key "K" on page 2 of the **User Guide**) to improve your experience. If you're interested in learning more, register at www.MGInAction.com

REVOLUTIONIZE **YOUR GAME.**

MGInAction.com
User Guide

KEY FEATURES

A. Open up your InAction Toolbar.

B. The website content is organized though different tabs located at the top of the page.

C. Shortcut to a pop up window that will load your video faster!

D. Open up a new window.

E. Add this video to your queue.

F. Add this video to your personal collection.

G. Keyword Searching allows you to search for videos specifically related to your search terms.

H. Search for techniques from the positional tree.

I. Load your favorite videos to your Queue so that you can watch them all in sequence without interruption. This is especially great for watching InAction clips!

J. Add videos to My Collection to create your own playlist.

I. If you use the mobile app, store your videos here for access on your mobile device.

K. Our new Mirroring feature allows you to watch Marcelo perform the technique to your preferred side.

L. The Loop switch allows you to watch the video continuously, so you can pick up all the details without having to hit play after each run through.

M. The full screen button will expand the video to fill your entire screen.

N. The Slow Motion feature allows you to run the video at 25%, 50%, or 75% of its actual speed. Use this function to study careful details as the technique is being performed.

O. Zoom in or out of any video that you would like to examine more closely.

P. Research Suggestions will recommend techniques based on what's playing in your video. This section assists you by developing the relationship between moves.

Q. Use Load to Queue for instantly viewing InAction clips of an individual technique.

MARCELO GARCIA'S

VIRTUAL ACADEMY + GRAPPLING DATABASE

www.MGInAction.com

ARM DRAGS

My grappling philosophy is to attack at all times, and the arm drag plays into that perfectly because it is a uniquely powerful technique. If I open a match with a successful double-leg takedown, I still have to pass the guard and mount before I can take the back. If I pull guard and successfully sweep my opponent with a butterfly sweep or a scissor sweep, I still have to pass the guard, mount, and set up a back-take. The arm drag, however, is a high-percentage shortcut to the back. In one move, I can skip having to pass the guard and having to fight for the mount. It feels like magic.

I have repeatedly proven that the arm drag is an effective technique, even against the best grapplers in the world. The arm drag was a key component to my success in the 2003 ADCC, and it is still an important part of my game today. I use the arm drag in virtually every competition I enter, whether it's the ADCC, the Mundials, Pan Ams, or another top-level competition. If it is successful, I am a few moves away from the rear naked choke.

Now that the arm drag is well known, competitors are aware that being caught with an arm drag quickly puts them behind in points and in danger of being submitted. Consequently, the simple act of attempting an arm drag gives me an advantage over my opponent. Our positioning may be neutral, but my opponent will worry about the arm drag for the rest of the match, forcing him into a defensive mind-set. If my opponent is defending, he cannot attack. I want to force him to panic, to make a mistake, to give me the opening I need to finish the fight.

THE STANDING ARM DRAG VS. THE SEATED ARM DRAG

In competition, I always prefer playing the top position to working from my back. On top, with gravity and mobility on my side, I can control and dominate my opponent. When my opponent is on his back, he is fighting to escape the pressure of my attacks. If I am attacking, he is forced to defend, and my attacks will always be stronger from the top.

Getting the top position, however, is not easy. As the sport continues to grow, the quality of competition grows as well. Olympic-grade wrestlers are entering jiu-jitsu competitions, and pure jiu-jitsu fighters are seeking out takedown specialists to improve their wrestling and takedown defense. As much as I would like to dominate the standing positions of a grappling match, shooting a single-leg takedown or working a standing arm drag on an NCAA champion is like attacking a bull head-on. The arm drag from the seated guard allows me to avoid the horns, neutralizing my opponent's strength and guiding the direction of the match into the positions where I am strong.

I used this same strategy against Mike van Arsdale in the 2003 ADCC. Early in the

match, it was clear that taking a shot on Arsdale was difficult and dangerous. With a lifetime of wrestling experience and a size advantage, Arsdale was well equipped to defend my takedown attempts, and if I tried to force a takedown, I risked Arsdale defending the attempt, reversing it, and establishing a dominant position. Instead of playing into Arsdale's strengths, I went to my seated guard and started attacking with a variety of techniques, all of which are in this book or in my previous book, The X-Guard. After a few attacks—butterfly sweeps, x-guard sweeps—I arm dragged Arsdale, took his back, and sank a rear naked choke.

So when I go to the seated guard, I'm not pulling guard in the way that many people think of pulling guard. I do not want to work a closed guard. I do not want to secure a deep half guard. When I pull guard, it is like an extended shot. I want to get inside, destabilize my opponent, and reverse the position as soon as possible. The principles of a takedown are there, but I am applying them in a different way and taking a different route to the top position. The arm drag is one of the core techniques for accomplishing this. If I get the arm drag, I am either taking the back or securing the top position. If my opponent defends the arm drag, he will almost always leave an opening for me to exploit, which will again take me to the top position.

INCORPORATING THE ARM DRAG

The system that I've developed for the arm drag fits perfectly into the x-guard system that I taught in my previous book. I can easily transition from the arm drag to the butterfly guard and into the x-guard, or my butterfly guard could give me the opening for an arm drag; all of the positions interconnect. But that is my game, and the way that I approach these positions may not fit your style. Fortunately, my arm drag system can easily be transplanted and incorporated into your personal game, regardless of whether or not the rest of your preferences resemble mine.

If you dedicate the time to drilling each technique, perfecting your speed and timing, the arm drag will soon become one of your favorite weapons. Your success with the arm drag will be compounded if you study the connection between each arm drag variation, so you can instinctually choose the right move for the situation and transition from counter to counter as your opponent attempts to defend.

I cannot overemphasize how important putting the hours into each technique truly is. As I described previously, my grappling philosophy is to always attack, to never give my opponent time to think. The flipside of this approach is that I will not have time to think either. To be a step ahead of my opponent, I have to already know my next move. The only way to accomplish this—and the only way to develop an exceptionally strong arm drag—is to know the common counters for the arm drag and the counters for those counters, all of which are addressed in my system.

The more you use the arm drag in the gym, the more comfortable you will be with flowing from technique to technique. Once you start frustrating your training partners with the arm drag, imagine how much success you will have in competition against an opponent that has no idea just how dangerous your arm drag can be.

THE GI DRAG

When I first started experimenting with the arm drag, I was in the process of developing my no-gi game. I had not yet dedicated the time to learning how to wrestle, and I was looking for ways to adapt what I already did in the gi to no gi. The arm drag became the jumping-off point for my wrestling techniques because the no-gi arm drag is very similar in terms of grips and mechanics to the gi variation of the arm drag. As I mastered the no-gi arm drag, I found that it was much quicker to execute because I did not need to fight for control of my opponent's sleeve, and I began to use the no-gi variation constantly, regardless of what type of competition I was in. The gi variation is still a part of my game because a strong grip on my opponent's sleeve gives me a great deal of control. Though you may end up preferring the no-gi arm drag that I teach in the next technique, starting where I started will help you to better understand the totality of my arm drag system.

Henrique is kneeling and is looking to set up a guard pass. I am in the seated guard position with my knees flared out and the outsides of my feet digging into the mat so that I can quickly scoot forward or away if necessary. To protect my legs, I position my elbows inside of my knees and float my hands directly above my ankles.

To initiate the gi variation of the arm drag, I latch on to Henrique's right wrist with my left hand.

As I continue to control his right wrist with my left hand, I shoot my right hand to the far side of his right wrist.

I gather a clump of sleeve fabric on the far side of Henrique's right wrist.

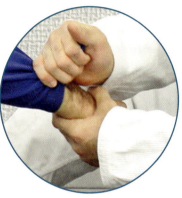

I establish a pistol grip on Henrique's right sleeve with my right hand. When I set this grip, I squeeze a clump of fabric in my hand, holding it like I would the handle of a gun. For my grip to be as secure as possible, it is important that I begin gathering fabric from the far side of his sleeve, not the near side.

With my right hand still controlling Henrique's right sleeve, I grab his triceps, just above his elbow, with my left hand. Note that the bottom of my right hand is positioned to the outside of his right wrist. This essential detail prevents him from grabbing my collar with his right hand.

I press off of the mat with my feet, driving my weight backward as I drag Henrique's right arm across my body and to the outside of my right hip. From here, I can finish the drag using any of the seated variations covered in this chapter.

BAITING WRIST CONTROL

I tend to use the no-gi variation of the arm drag more often because grabbing my opponent's wrist tends to be much faster than setting a sleeve grip, especially if my opponent and I are standing. Even with the additional speed of the no-gi arm drag at my disposal, the majority of my opponents are well aware that I like to use arm drags, so they are especially careful to protect their arms and their wrists. To establish wrist control against such an opponent, I have developed techniques to bait or trick my opponent into giving me his wrist. In the sequences below, I teach you three options for establishing wrist control. In the first, you allow your opponent to grab your wrist and use his grip to initiate the arm drag. In the next option, you trick your opponent into reaching for your wrist, bringing his wrist within range for you to grab. Remember, speed is a significant factor in grip fighting. To be effective with these tactics, you need to dedicate the time to drilling and perfecting the movements.

Henrique and I are standing, fighting for grips.

I attempt to grab Henrique's right wrist with my left hand, but he immediately pulls his arm back to hide from my grip.

Since Henrique is too quick, I decide to bait him into giving me his wrist by extending my left arm, offering him a grip that is too good to resist. Henrique falls for it and grabs my left wrist with his right hand.

I swing my left arm across my body, toward my right hip. Henrique clings to my right wrist as I move my arm, allowing me to execute the arm drag without ever having to grab his wrist. As I drag his arm, I step my left foot forward next to his right foot and begin to shoot my right hand under his right arm.

I latch on to Henrique's right triceps with my right hand and connect my right shoulder to his. From this position, I can execute any variation of the arm drag that I choose.

BAITING WRIST CONTROL OPTION 2

Henrique and I are standing, looking for grips and for takedown opportunities.

I attempt to grab Henrique's right wrist with my left hand, but he quickly jerks his arm away to defend.

Accepting that Henrique is too quick, I extend my left arm slightly, baiting him to grab my left wrist with his right hand.

MG IN ACTION

When Henrique reaches to grip my left wrist with his right hand, I pull my left arm away.

In one motion, I latch on to his right wrist with my left hand and step my left foot forward as I reach to grab his right tricps with my right hand.

I control Henrique's right tricep with my right hand, passing his right arm across my body as I press my right shoulder into his right shoulder. I am now in a great position to complete the arm drag.

ALTERNATE OPTION: CROSS GRIP

I could also use the same bait to establish a cross grip with my right hand and then pass Henrique's right wrist to my left hand.

I grab Henrique's right wrist with my right hand.

Without releasing wrist control, I reach to grab his right wrist with my left hand.

I transfer Henrique's right wrist to my left hand. With this grip established, I can now execute an arm drag.

NEAR GRIP ARM DRAG TO BACK CONTROL (STANDING)

When you use the arm drag from the standing position, the ideal result would be a quick and easy transition to the back body lock or to back control. Unfortunately, when you attempt to rip your opponent off balance with the arm drag, he will almost always resist by retracting his arm and driving his weight away. As a smaller grappler, I always assume that my opponent will be larger, stronger, and even faster, so my solution is not to hit the arm drag with more force or with more speed. Instead, I sit my butt to the mat, using my body weight to haul my opponent forward on to his knees. From his knees, he is less mobile, and if I succeed in dragging his arm across my body, he is in a vulnerable position. When this technique is performed correctly, you will nullify your opponent's physical advantages and create an opening to take the back. I used this same approach in the 2003 ADCC against Vitor "Shaolin" Ribeiro. Ribeiro was quick, explosive, and strong. When he resisted my standing back-take, I dragged him to the ground, took his back, and set my choke.

Henrique and I start standing, battling for grips.

Since Henrique's right foot is forward, I latch on to his right wrist with my left hand.

Then, in one motion, I step my left foot next to his right foot, cup his right triceps—just above his right elbow—with my right hand, and guide his right arm across my body with my left hand. This combination of movements connects my right shoulder to his right shoulder and positions his right wrist to the outside of my right wrist, which are essential components of a successful arm drag.

I attempt to force Henrique to step forward so I can transition to his back, but he resists by basing out and pulling his arm back. Before he can rip his arm free, I step my right foot between his feet, and I press my right shoulder into his right shoulder. If I don't put weight on his shoulder, his base will be too strong, and he will be able to defend.

To bring Henrique to the mat, I sit back, driving off the mat with my feet for extra momentum. Notice that I am still cupping his right arm with my right hand and that my right shoulder is still attached to his right shoulder. Space is my enemy in this step.

As I land, I roll to my back and kick my left leg into the air. As you can see, I maintain control of Henrique's right arm with my right hand and keep my right leg positioned between his legs. The former prevents him from posturing up, and the latter allows me to secure a leg hook as I sit up to take control of his back.

I swing my left leg down to the mat and pull on Henrique's right arm with my right hand to generate enough momentum to sit up.

As I sit up, I curl my left leg behind me.

I press off of the mat with my left foot and drive my chest into Henrique's upper back. As I begin to take his back, I snake my right arm in front of his right shoulder and down his chest, pointing my right hand toward his left hip.

To prevent Henrique from escaping, I reach under his armpit with my left hand and grab my right wrist, establishing seatbelt control as I use my arms to squeeze my chest into his upper back.

In order to take Henrique's back, I must first collapse his base. To accomplish this, I fall toward my right shoulder and wrap my right leg around his right leg, stretching it and blocking him from hopping his right knee forward to recover his balance. It's important to note that you want to keep your seatbelt grip as tight as possible. If your grip is loose, your opponent will turn into you and establish top control.

IN ACTION

I continue with the roll and land on my right side. My seatbelt grip squeezes into Henrique's chest, keeping my back control secure. My right leg, which was between his legs when I first dragged him to the ground, now becomes my first hook.

While maintaining a tight seatbelt control, I maneuver my left leg over and in front of Henrique's left leg.

I set my left calf against the left side of Henrique's groin, establishing my second back hook and securing back control.

NEAR GRIP ARM DRAG TO BACK (FROM SITTING)

The seated guard is an integral part of my game. From the seated guard, I can transition to butterfly guard or x-guard, both of which are powerful sweeping positions that I taught in my first book. Because my opponent is forced to attempt to pass my guard, I can typically capitalize on his aggression and set up a variety of different sweeps. However, once an opponent realizes how dangerous my seated guard is, he sometimes becomes timid and hesitates to pass aggressively. In this situation, attacking with the arm drag is a great way to open up my opponent and move to a dominant position. In the previous technique, I attempted the arm drag from standing and countered my opponent's resistance by using my body weight to drag him to the mat. In this technique, the same principle is at work, except that I am executing the arm drag from the seated guard. To generate the same momentum with a seated drag as a standing drag, I need to use the power of my legs to throw my body weight away from my opponent to pull him off balance.

I am in the seated guard, my knees flared out, the outsides of my feet digging into the mat. I position my hands directly over top of my feet to protect my ankles. I know that Henrique is going to attempt a guard pass, and if I allow him to control my ankles, he has a much better chance of beating my guard.

As Henrique reaches to grab my left ankle with his right hand, I latch on to his right wrist with my left hand. Controlling his sleeve is tempting, but establishing a proper sleeve grip often takes too much time.

Without releasing Henrique's right wrist, I step my left foot to the outside of his right knee.

4

I drag Henrique's right arm across my body with my left hand as I shoot my right hand under his right arm and cup his right triceps.

5

When Henrique attempts to pull his right arm away from my body, I use his energy to sit forward, lifting my butt off of the mat and driving my chest toward his right shoulder.

6

Still maintaining my grips on Henrique's arm, I kick off of my feet, launching myself backward.

Henrique falls forward, posting on his forearms as my back lands on the mat. Without pausing, I use the momentum of the arm drag to kick my left leg into the air. Remember, it is imperative that I continue to cup his right triceps with my right hand and that my right leg remains between his legs.

To sit up, I swing my left leg to the mat like a pendulum and pull on Henrique's elbow with my right hand.

As I sit up, I turn my chest toward Henrique's back and set my right arm over his right shoulder, setting up the seatbelt grip.

Throwing my left arm over Henrique's back, I glue my chest to the middle of his upper back and grab my right wrist with my left hand, locking the seatbelt.

Pushing off of the mat with my right foot, I roll over my right shoulder to collapse Henrique's base, landing on my right side with my first hook already set.

While squeezing my chest to Henrique's back, I swing my left leg into the air.

I secure my second hook by setting my left foot in front of Henrique's left thigh.

ARM DRAG TO SINGLE POSITION TO BACK CONTROL

When you initiate the standing arm drag, you must be ready to counter your opponent's attempts to defend. If you succeed in dragging him forward to the mat, he could attempt to post on his hands and quickly bear-crawl away from you to protect his back. Talented grapplers will often do this because they understand the power of the arm drag, and they will do everything that they can to avoid having their back taken. To counter this defense, you cannot transition directly to the back as we did before because your opponent's back will be too far away. Instead, attack his nearest leg with a single-leg takedown. If you are fast enough, you can achieve the single-leg position before your opponent stands, and you can jump onto his back. If you transition to the single-leg position and your opponent stands, either transition to the back body lock or work to finish the single-leg takedown. In this sequence, you take the back. I will cover strategies for other scenarios later in the book.

Henrique and I start standing, each of us looking to establish a dominant grip.

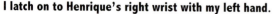
I latch on to Henrique's right wrist with my left hand.

3

I reach across with my right hand and cup Henrique's right triceps as I step my left foot forward.

4

I step my right foot forward as well, planting it between Henrique's legs. As I move toward him, I drag his right arm to the outside of my right hip.

5

To pull him off balance, I sit back, maintaining my grips on Henrique's right arm to bring him with me.

As I land, I notice that Henrique is posting on his hands instead of his forearms to begin to run away from my back-take.

Without releasing my grip on Henrique's right triceps, I immediately swing my left arm around the back of his right knee, turning my chest to face his right hip.

I use my left arm to hug my chest to Henrique's right leg as I shift onto my right hip.

I post my right hand on the mat and drive my head into Henrique's right hip. Notice that my right leg is still between his legs in this step.

In one motion, I rotate my hips toward the mat and step up onto my left foot to begin standing. As I make that transition, I hook Henrique's right foot in the bend of my left knee to limit his ability to escape and to increase the power my single-leg takedown.

I stand, hugging Henrique's leg with both arms. In some cases, I will attempt to finish the single-leg takedown by sprawling my weight back, but against a larger opponent or an opponent with a strong base, I use the single-leg to transition to a back body lock. If he stands, finishing the single-leg will be my only choice, but I can prevent him from doing that by keeping his right leg elevated and by shoving him forward when he attempts to straighten his back.

I hop forward and wrap both of my arms around Henrique's waist, keeping my hips slightly below his to keep my base strong. As I come forward, I favor his right side, the same side that I was attacking with the single-leg, by planting my right foot between his right foot and his right hand.

I jump onto Henrique's back, reaching around his chest with my right arm and reaching under his armpit with my left arm while balancing on my right foot. As always, I attach my chest and shoulder to his upper back and squeeze with the seatbelt grip.

To roll Henrique over, I swing my left leg toward his spine and throw my right foot under his hips, planting it in the center point between his hands and his feet.

Pressing off of the mat slightly with my right foot, I squeeze the seatbelt grip as tight as I can and fall over my right shoulder, dragging Henrique with me. I land on my right side with my right foot positioned as my first hook.

I swing my left leg over Henrique's left leg to establish my second hook. I can now fight to finish the match with a rear naked choke.

HELPFUL HINT

MGInAction is designed to weave theory and practice together for our members. Study the 'Instructionals' to see how a particular technique is broken down; then view the 'InAction' clips to see it in practice. As you watch a technique being executed in real time, you can witness and absorb the details and nuances that are needed to make it successful.

MGInAction.com

ARM DRAG LEG TRIP TO BACK CONTROL

When faced with a very quick opponent, you may not have time to transition to the single-leg position. If you attempted the previous technique and your opponent simply ran from you, or if you suspect that your opponent is extremely fast, couple the standing arm drag with a leg trip to slow him down. A leg trip will force him to recover his balance and momentarily shift his focus away from defending his back. Other than the addition of the leg trip, the rest of the technique is the same, but I cannot stress the importance of the leg trip enough. By countering his speed with a tactical maneuver like a leg trip, you conserve energy and use his strengths against him. Trying to beat speed with speed will quickly tire you out and leave you vulnerable. Win the fight with your mind.

Henrique and I are standing, fighting for the takedown.

I latch on to Henrique's right wrist with my left hand.

I step my left foot forward and cup Henrique's right elbow with my right hand as I pass his right arm across my body, connecting my shoulder to his shoulder.

Henrique resists the arm drag, so I begin to sit my weight back to continue the arm drag. When I attempted this same arm drag earlier in the match, he was too fast and was able to run away from me before I could take his back or establish a single-leg position.

To slow Henrique, I extend my right leg as I fall, setting my right ankle in front of his left ankle to trip him.

6

The trip works. Henrique stumbles and scrambles to recover his balance, momentarily forgetting to protect his back. Without hesitating, I turn my chest toward his right hip and reach for the back of his right knee with my left arm.

7

Turning onto my right hip, I wrap my left arm around the back of Henrique's right leg. Notice that his right foot is trapped in the bend of my right knee, just like it was in the previous technique.

8

Before Henrique can think to run, I hug his right leg to my chest, rotate my hips toward the mat, and step on to my left foot to begin the transition to the single-leg. As I stand, I trap his right leg between my legs.

MG IN ACTION

I step up onto my right foot to stand, hugging Henrique's right leg with both arms.

Shucking Henrique's right leg between my legs as I step my right foot forward and wrap my arms around his waist, securing the back body lock.

In one motion, I jump onto Henrique's back, plant my chest between his shoulder blades, and balance on my right foot. As my chest moves into position, my right arm loops over his right shoulder and my left arm shoots under his left armpit.

I grab my right wrist with my left hand to secure seatbelt control, and I swing my left leg under Henrique's hips to begin rolling him to the mat.

I roll over my right shoulder and push off of the mat to collapse Henrique's base, landing on my right side with my right foot set as my first back hook.

I maneuver my left foot on top of Henrique's left thigh to establish my second hook and to stabilize back control.

ARM DRAG TO JUMPING BACK ATTACK

Using your body weight to augment the leverage of the arm drag is a great way to increase your success with the technique. Sometimes, however, an opponent will be so large and so strong that he can remain standing when you throw yourself backward for the arm drag. I faced this dilemma multiple times when competing in the absolute division of various tournaments, and I knew that I needed a strategy for dealing with this problem. Now, when I attempt the standing arm drag and my opponent does not fall to the mat with me, I use his resistance to launch myself forward and swing onto his back. As you practice this technique, learn to feel your opponent's resistance and strive to time your jumping back-take with the retraction of his arm. If you do that, he will do most of the work for you and pull you onto his back.

Henrique and I are fighting for a takedown, and I grip his right wrist with my left hand.

I reach across and cup Henrique's right triceps with my right hand as I step forward with my left foot, connecting my right shoulder to his right shoulder. If I suspect that my opponent will completely resist the standing arm drag, I set my right hand as deep as possible, almost as though I were trying to cup his biceps. A deeper grip will lessen the likelihood of his arm slipping free when I fall.

3

I step my right foot between Henrique's legs, preparing to throw myself backward for the arm drag.

4

When I throw myself backward for the arm drag, Henrique remains standing.

5

The instant Henrique retracts his right arm in attempt to rip free, I pull on his right arm with both hands to come up to my feet.

MG IN ACTION

6

Without pausing, I jump into the air as I swing my body behind Henrique. Notice that my right arm naturally slides in front of his right shoulder as I make the transition to back control while I loop my left hand, which is no longer controlling his right wrist, toward his left armpit.

7

To secure the back position, I set my left foot against the inside of Henrique's left thigh, I lock the seatbelt grip, and I glue my chest to his upper back. In order to maintain this position, I must maintain a strong squeeze with my arms and not allow my feet to drift below his knees.

FAILED ARM DRAG TO DOUBLE-LEG TAKEDOWN

The arm drag has become a popular technique among competitive grapplers, so when you attempt an arm drag on an opponent, he will likely divine your intentions and become wary of your offense. He knows that if you complete the arm drag, he will be in a bad position. You can use this fear to your advantage by making him hypersensitive to your arm drag attempts. Using the arm drag as a distraction, you can trick your opponent into yanking his arm away from your hands. While the arm drag will no longer be available, your opponent's hands and arms will be away from his hips, leaving him susceptible to a double-leg takedown. Train yourself to recognize this opening so that you can capitalize on the opportunity without hesitation. If your opponent begins to fend off the double-leg, use the strategies and techniques contained in the takedown chapter to remain aggressive and continue attacking.

Henrique and I are squared off, looking for grips and for takedowns.

I latch on to Henrique's right wrist with my left hand to set up an arm drag.

3

I shoot my right hand toward his right triceps.

4

Henrique, wary of my arm drag, rips his right arm away from my hands.

5

Without hesitating, I sink my hips to change levels and drive my right knee forward to begin shooting for a double-leg.

6

I plant my right knee between Henrique's legs, set my head against the outside of his right hip, and wrap my arms around his legs, hugging my chest to his thighs.

7

I continue the momentum of my shot by stepping my left foot forward. Notice that my back is straight, creating a strong posture.

8

As I drive off of the mat to stand, I look to the ceiling and turn to the right somewhat to create additional leverage. As I complete this movement, I hug Henrique's legs as tightly as possible to prevent him from sprawling.

Once I stand, I shoot forward and swing Henrique's legs between mine as I twist to my right slightly.

I land on top of Henrique.

I lower my hips and settle my weight to secure the top position. From here, I can work to achieve a more dominant position and finish the fight.

MG FAST FACT

Arm Drags are a great tool for developing a solid offensive game from seated guard. Many attacks rely on a counter or setting the opponent up to make a mistake, however this technique forces the opponent into a defensive position.

On MGInAction:
1. Search for videos using the term 'Arm Drag'.
2. Go to the 'InAction' tab.
3. On the top left corner of the page you will see 'Load to Queue'.
4. Click on it to watch all related 'Arm Drag InAction' clips consecutively.

MGInAction.com

FAILED ARM DRAG TO SINGLE-LEG (FROM SITTING)

In the previous technique, I used a failed arm drag from standing to transition to a double-leg take-down, but the same concept can be applied to the seated guard. If I am working from the seated guard while my opponent is attempting to pass, I can threaten the arm drag, which can create an opening for me to attack with a single-leg takedown if he exposes his legs by yanking his arms away from my hands. Never forget that simply threatening the arm drag from any position forces your opponent into a defensive mind-set. If you drill this technique and make it instinctual, a failed arm drag won't be a failure at all; it will have just taken you in a different—but still very advantageous—direction. You will find yourself hitting this transition constantly, making you a much more aggressive and dangerous grappler.

I am in a seated guard, and Henrique is standing, attempting to pass. My knees are bent and flared out, the outsides of my feet are digging into the mat, and my hands are positioned directly above my feet to protect my ankles. If he wants to pass my guard, he has to come forward and secure a grip.

Henrique reaches with his right hand to establish a grip, and I immediately grab his right wrist with my left hand.

While maintaining control of Henrique's wrist with my left hand, I reach across and cup his right elbow with my right hand. Even though he is probably too far away for my arm drag to be a serious threat, the attempt itself can be enough to create an opening for another attack.

Henrique senses that he is in danger and yanks his arm free, which creates a momentary hole in his defense.

Before Henrique can recover his posture, I scoot forward and wrap my left arm around his right leg, aiming my head to the inside of his right thigh.

I post my right hand on the mat as I drive my chest toward Henrique's knee. It is important that I do not linger in this position for long.

Pushing off of my right hand, I swivel my hips to the outside of Henrique's right leg, trapping his right ankle in the crook of my right leg as I make the transition. With my chest pressed into the side of his right knee, I am relatively safe from counters. If I face his knee, he can easily counter my single-leg with guard passes and with submissions.

With my right hand still posted on the mat, I execute a technical standup, swinging my right leg through the arch created by my left leg and right arm. As I stand, I do my best to keep Henrique's right leg trapped between my legs.

Once I stand, I wrap both of my arms around Henrique's leg. I press my head against the inside of his thigh to optimize the leverage of my single-leg takedown.

To begin the single-leg takedown, I step my right foot forward, aligning my legs.

I then step my left leg back.

I swing my hips to my left and down to the mat while pressing my head against Henrique's right thigh. I keep my single-leg position as tight as possible throughout the takedown.

I land on top of Henrique, straddling his right leg.

To secure the top position, I set my right knee on the mat and settle my weight. I can now begin to pass his half guard.

WEAK-SIDE ARM DRAG TO DOUBLE-LEG

Like most people, I have a dominant side and a nondominant side. My arm drags are strongest when I am moving to my left, attacking my opponent's right arm. If I attack his opposite arm, I rarely complete the technique by taking his back. On that side, I feel much more comfortable using the arm drag to clear a path for a double-leg takedown. Perfecting the arm drag to the back on both sides is undoubtedly worthwhile, so feel free to use the previous techniques on the opposite side. At the same time, learning to use the arm drag to set up the double-leg will also be useful and is applicable to both sides. Find what works best for you, and use my techniques as a launch pad for developing your own jiu-jitsu game.

Henrique and I are both fighting for a takedown. I attempted to attack Henrique's right arm with an arm drag, but he was too good at defending. I decide to change my strategy and attack his left arm by latching on to his left wrist with my right hand.

As I swing his left arm across my body with my right hand, I shoot my left hand under his left arm and cup his left triceps.

Since this is my weak side, I am not comfortable using the arm drag to take Henrique's back, so I use the arm drag to clear a path for a double-leg takedown by flinging his left arm to my left with both hands.

 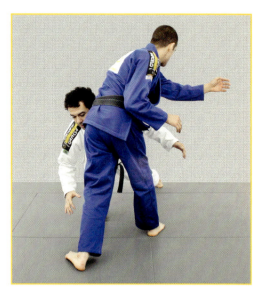

Before Henrique can reestablish posture, I sink my hips to change levels and shoot forward, driving my right knee between his legs.

 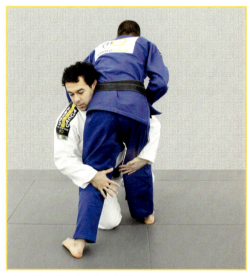

As I plant my left knee between Henrique's legs, I wrap my arms around his legs, hooking the backs of his knees.

Still moving forward, I step up onto my left foot. Notice how there is very little space between Henrique and me. The deeper I penetrate with my shot, the better.

7

I suck Henrique's legs toward my hips with my arms as I drive off of the mat with my feet and twist to my left.

8

I follow through with the takedown, following Henrique to the mat.

9

Henrique lands on his back, and I land on top of him.

10

I pull my knees in to settle my base and to prepare to pass Henrique's half guard.

ESTABLISHING BACK CONTROL

The arm drag will put you in position to take the back, but securing back control is never easy. Your opponent knows that he loses points for giving up the position, and more importantly, he knows that if you do take his back you are very close to finishing the fight with a submission. He will do everything he can to protect himself, using every counter and escape he knows to stop you from achieving your goal. If your opponent is skilled at escaping and countering, taking the back can result in you losing position. I see it all the time: a competitor invests a great deal of effort in getting to his opponent's back, but he loses the position at the last moment and ends up on the bottom.

I used to struggle with this same problem, so I obsessed over the dynamics of the back control position and experimented with various strategies and positional variations to find the best possible ways of taking the back. After much trial and error, I discovered the back body lock position and developed a strategy for using the back body lock to bridge the gap between being behind my opponent and transitioning to his back.

Most grapplers at the time thought that the best option from the back body lock was a suplex, which to me, required too much strength and effort. Once on the back, I decided that having one overhook and one underhook was preferable to having double underhooks. I later realized that setting my first hook was never nearly as challenging as setting the second hook, so I perfected a series of techniques to establish and maintain my second hook.

Once I knew that my back control was dangerous, I began to hunt for the back anytime my opponent turned his chest to the mat, even in positions where many grapplers at the time typically wouldn't have thought about taking the back. The more confident I became in my ability to take the back, the more aggressively I fought for the position, which dramatically increased my ability to control and finish matches.

back-take. I can use the back body lock as a launch pad for jumping to the back, or I can use it to drag my opponent to the mat before I attempt to take the back. How I use the back body lock depends on how my opponent defends, and having the ability to choose how I attack significantly improved my finish rate. If you want your back-taking arsenal to be well rounded, you will need the control that the back body lock provides, especially if you plan to master the arm drag.

THE BACK BODY LOCK

On my quest to master back control, I found that if my opponent stood as I transitioned to his back, I could not simply jump to his back and set my hooks. Doing so gave him too much space to counter. And as I developed my arm drag system, it became more and more apparent that I needed a strategy for establishing back control from the standing position. If I did not develop a dependable game plan for securing the back, all of the time that I had invested in the arm drag would have been time wasted.

The back body lock was the answer I was looking for.

When I get to my opponent's back and we are standing, the back body lock gives me the ability to control him and set up a methodical

THE SEATBELT

The traditional approach for controlling the back is to use double underhooks, gripping both of your opponent's lapels if he's wearing a gi. This position is great for controlling your opponent's movement and preventing him from escaping, but using double underhooks has a few inherent problems. When you remove an underhook to attack your opponent, with a rear naked choke for example, the distance that your arm must travel to attack the neck is great, giving your opponent time to defend. Worse yet, he can use this transition as an opening for an escape.

Using one overhook and one underhook, a position I call over-under control, or "the seatbelt," solved the problems I had with using double underhooks to control the back. As long as I squeezed my chest to my opponent's upper back, the seatbelt gave me just as much positional security as the double underhooks, and with my overhook ready to jam into my opponent's neck as soon as there was an opening, my submission rate increased exponentially. When I realized how much success I was having with the seatbelt, I decided that the seatbelt was indeed superior to having double underhooks, and I proved it by using the seatbelt to finish match after match with the rear naked choke. To be successful with the seatbelt, you need to be aware of a few nuances that can be the difference between winning the fight by submission or losing back control and ending up on the bottom:

-When you use the seatbelt, always use your over-under control to squeeze your chest to your opponent's back. In terms of control, this squeeze is more important than the hooks. While the hooks certainly help you maintain back control, having a strong seatbelt will allow you to continue attacking the back even if your opponent is good at shaking off your legs.

-When you establish the seatbelt, always grip your overhook wrist with your underhook hand using a ball and socket style grip to hide your overhook hand underneath your underhook hand and wrist. Gripping the wrist of your choking arm makes it more difficult for your opponent to control your choking arm, which will save you a lot of struggle in the long run.

-If his neck is exposed, attack it, even if you do not have the hooks. I use the seatbelt because I want to be able to choke my opponent the second he leaves his neck exposed. I will talk more about the details of the rear naked choke in the next chapter, but start hunting the neck as you develop your back-control game.

-When you lay your opponent on his side, always try to lie on your overhook side. That way, you can easily remove your underhook to finish the rear naked choke. Be aware that if you only have one hook in, you have more control over your opponent if you are lying on the side of your hook, so try to set your first hook on the side of your overhook arm.

-If you actively look to establish the seatbelt every time your opponent exposes his back, you will find yourself taking the back more often and more consistently. Develop your squeeze, and use the techniques in this chapter to maximize the effectiveness of the seatbelt.

THE HOOKS

I mentioned before that it is more important to establish the seatbelt than the hooks, but that does not mean that I do not need the hooks. I just prefer to look for the seatbelt and then the hooks because if I lose the hooks, I can use the seatbelt to reset my position and reposition my feet. The hooks are still a very important part of controlling the back, and you need a strategy for setting and maintaining the hooks if you want a dangerous back game. It has been my experience that once you have the seatbelt, setting the first hook is relatively easy. The true battle is establishing the second hook.

In this chapter, I demonstrate multiple techniques for smashing through your opponent's last-ditch efforts to block your second hook and for preventing your opponent from escaping once you do have the hooks, but to make the most of these techniques you need to implement two principles:

-Always lie on the side of your first hook. Ideally, this should be the same side as your overhook. If you lie on the side where you don't have a hook, your opponent will quickly turn his back to the mat and shrimp out.

-When you are fighting for the second hook, do not forget about your ultimate goal, which is finishing the rear naked choke. If at any moment your opponent exposes his neck, attack.

These techniques are organized as part of a linear system so that you can see how each technique connects, but do not allow that to limit your thinking. As soon as you lose one of your hooks, immediately go back to your techniques for establishing the second hook. It does not matter how you lost the second hook: your opponent could have shrugged it off or maybe you removed it yourself to attempt to trap his arm or to counter his bridge escape. Regardless of the specifics, you always need to be prepared to go back to your techniques for establishing the second hook if necessary. With that said, the second hook is not necessarily vital in terms of control and finishing. The more I play the back position, the more I find myself preferring to attack with the seatbelt and one hook, leaving my other leg free to stifle my opponent's counters by hooking his legs or by trapping his arms. This is an advanced way of approaching back control, and it hinges on your proficiency

with the seatbelt. At first, it may be wise to play a more traditional back control game, hunting for both hooks and fighting to finish from there, but once you get your points for the back mount and as you become dangerous with your seatbelt, begin to experiment fighting with only one hook.

COUNTERTACTICS

In my mind, the back is the most vulnerable part of the human body. Your arms and hands are positioned in front of you to protect your chest and face, and you cannot easily reach behind you to protect your back. If your opponent's back is not on the mat, he is vulnerable. This, of course, was a gradual revelation for me. The more confident I became in my ability to control and submit from the back, the more aggressively I hunted for the position. My arm drag system continued to improve, but I was not satisfied with just using the arm drag to take the back, and I quickly exhausted the traditional approaches for taking the back, so I began to experiment. If my leg was between my opponent's legs, I started to think of that position as already having my first hook. Soon, I developed a slew of new ways to take the back. Some of them may seem unorthodox, but once you are aware that the option is there, what once seemed unorthodox will become a regular part of your game.

BREAKING WRIST CONTROL

The back body lock is a powerful position. It is a great staging position for setting up a back-take or setting up a takedown. For me, I am always looking to take the back, and that means securing the seatbelt. To do that, my arms need to be free, but my opponents tend to attack my wrists to break my grip and to counter with kimuras. You are likely to encounter the same reaction when you begin to incorporate the back body lock into your game, so having a strategy for freeing your arms is important. If you are unable to escape your opponent's grips, you will never be able to take his back and set the rear naked choke. In this technique, you knock your opponent off balance, forcing him to release your wrists to regain his stability.

I have Henrique in a back body lock. He is gripping my wrists, trying to counter the position.

I bend my knees and jerk my weight backward to pull Henrique off balance.

Henrique releases my wrists and throws his arms forward to keep from falling on to his butt.

OUTSIDE LEG TRIP (BREAKING WRIST CONTROL OPTION 2)

In many cases, jerking your opponent backward will be enough to break his grips on your wrists. An exceptionally strong and experienced grappler, however, may be able to maintain his balance without having to release your wrists. You cannot accept defeat. You must continue to work to free your wrists. In this technique, you attack with an outside leg trip. If your opponent is foolish enough to cling to your wrists as he falls, his face will slam into the mat. Most of the time, your opponent will instinctively release your wrists to post, which is precisely what you want. With your arms free, you can transition to a back take and work to finish the fight.

I am controlling Henrique with a back body lock, but he is gripping my wrists to prevent me from jumping onto his back.

I attempt to free my wrists by yanking Henrique backward, but he is strong and has good balance.

Recognizing that my first grip-breaking option has failed, I shuffle my feet to my right.

Wrapping my right leg around Henrique's right leg, I scoop his right leg backward to threaten an outside leg trip.

To defend the takedown, Henrique posts on his hands, freeing my wrists and giving me a path to his back.

SEATBELT TO BACK CONTROL

Once my wrists are free, I can use the back body lock to transition to back control, which can be done in a few different ways. In this technique, I jump onto my opponent's back while he remains standing. For this transition to be successful, it must be quick. If done slowly, your opponent could have time to defend and counter. Do not be intimidated by this technique. If you practice it with a partner, you can develop your timing and confidence to the point that you naturally jump onto your opponent's back without hesitation. A word of caution: jumping onto your opponent's back may be unwise if your opponent is taller than you. The greater the height difference, the more distance you must travel to set the seatbelt. Consequently, a taller opponent has more time to defend the transition. To compensate for a height disadvantage, use the crab ride, which is the technique that I teach next.

I have Henrique in a back body lock.

I sink my hips and bend my knees, preparing to launch myself into the air to take Henrique's back.

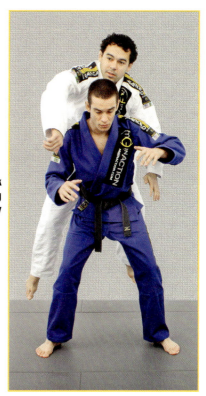

In one motion, I release my back body lock and jump onto Henrique's back, swooping my right arm over his right shoulder and my left arm under his left armpit.

While I establish seatbelt control with my arms, I pinch my knees against Henrique's hips. Once the seatbelt is set, I set one hook at a time. If I try to set my hooks too soon, I could lose the back position. I set the seatbelt first because the seatbelt is more important than the hooks.

CRAB RIDE TO BACK CONTROL

Jumping to my opponent's back from the back body lock is an excellent way to transition to the back, but against a larger opponent, the distance from his hips to his back may be too great to travel in one explosive movement. When I faced Ricco Rodriguez in the Absolute Division of the 2005 ADCC, I was faced with this same dilemma. Getting Rodriguez in the back body lock took a great deal of effort, and I knew that jumping directly to his back was too risky. I didn't want to release my back body lock until I was absolutely sure that I could establish seatbelt control, so I attacked Rodriguez with the crab ride instead, planting my feet in the backs of his knees to collapse his base. I brought him to the mat, nullified his size advantage, and took his back. This is a great technique, and it is one of my favorites.

I have Henrique in a back body lock, and I am concerned that I will lose my position if I jump to his back.

While tightly squeezing the back body lock, I bend my knees and sink my hips.

I maintain the back body lock, and hop up, setting both of my feet in the backs of Henrique's knees, pointing my toes out.

I pull Henrique's hips backward with my arms and extend my legs straight out, forcing him to fall.

When we land on the mat, I immediately straighten my legs to stretch out Henrique's legs, momentarily reducing his mobility.

Moving quickly, I release the back body lock and begin to transition to the seatbelt grip by setting my right arm over Henrique's right shoulder and snaking my left arm under his left armpit.

I grab my right wrist with my left hand, squeezing with my arms to press my chest against Henrique's back, securing the seatbelt.

Since my right arm is over Henrique's shoulder, I maneuver my right foot over his right thigh, establishing my first hook.

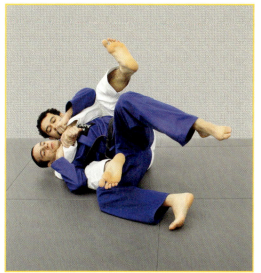

With my first hook set, I use my seatbelt control to drag Henrique onto his right side, the side of my overhook.

I snake my left foot to the top of Henrique's left thigh to set my second hook. I now have his back and can work for the submission.

MG FAST FACT

Seatbelt Control is the most important part of maintaining back control. Keep this in mind as you study the techniques in this chapter.

MGInAction.com

OVER-THE-BACK ATTACK OPTION 1

If your opponent posts on all fours to defend against the outside leg trip or to defend against the crab ride, jumping to his back is now an option regardless of his height. The key to this transition is to not overshoot your opponent's back. You may think that you need to launch yourself forward, but using too much energy will work against you. Once your hips are above your opponent's hips, gravity will do the rest if you aim your chest properly, and you use the seatbelt to attach yourself to your opponent's back. As it is with any technique, practice and repetition are essential for developing your timing and coordination. If you struggle with this technique at first, do not get frustrated. It took me some time to perfect this transition as well.

I have Henrique in a back body lock. He is defending by bending over and posting on his hands. I want to transition to his back, but he has positioned his elbows close to his knees to block me from setting my hooks.

I bend my knees and sink my hips to stretch Henrique out and to set up my back-take.

To open a path for me to take Henrique's back, I shuffle my feet to my right as though I were going to set up an outside leg trip, and I use the back body lock to push him forward, forcing him to adjust his hand placement to maintain his balance.

Since I chose to favor Henrique's right side, I throw my right arm over his right shoulder and my left arm under his left arm pit. If you look closely at the photographs, you can see that I jump more upward than I do forward. My goal is to get my hips above his hips. From that point, gravity will slide my chest down his spine to his upper back.

I lock the seatbelt grip as my chest falls toward Henrique's shoulder blades. I squeeze immediately with my arms and with my knees to halt my forward momentum, sticking myself to his back. It's important to note that I tuck my head against his head and leave it there for the rest of the technique. If I lift my head and he rolls forward, my face will smash into the mat.

6

Continuing to squeeze my chest to Henrique's upper back with my arms, I maneuver my right foot over his right thigh and between his legs. I curl my toes around the back of his right thigh to create a deep hook, which helps me to maintain my position.

7

I snake my left foot over Henrique's left thigh and between his legs, curling my toes around the back of his left thigh to create a hook as deep as my first. I now have full control of his back and can work to finish the fight.

OVER-THE-BACK ATTACK OPTION 2

Jumping to the back of a bent-over opponent is not without risks. With so much of your weight falling forward, your opponent could attempt to counter by rolling you over his shoulder, leaving you on your back working from your guard. If you have the seatbelt, you can use that control to recover and reset your back control. This is one of the reasons why I advocate the seatbelt over double underhooks. If you ever lose your back hooks, the seatbelt allows you to remain attached to your opponent's back and provides enough stability for you to retake his back. As long as you keep your chest pressed against your opponent's shoulder blades and do not allow him to turn into you, you can use the seatbelt to attack with back-take after back-take.

I have already opened Henrique up by shuffling my feet to my right and shoving him forward.

I bend my knees, preparing to jump onto Henrique's back.

Since Henrique's right shoulder is closest to me, I swim my right arm over his right shoulder and my left arm under his left armpit as I jump onto his back.

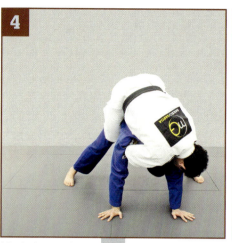

I lock the seatbelt grip and squeeze my knees to attach myself to Henrique's back, but I feel myself slipping forward.

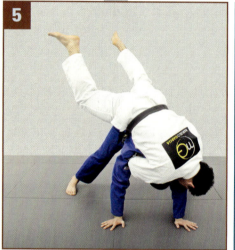

To prevent myself from falling to an unfavorable position, I kick my feet into the air and swing my legs to my right, toward the same side as my overhook. Even though I am hopping to Henrique's side, I continue to plant my chest firmly against his shoulder blades.

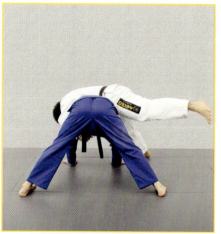

I plant my feet perpendicular to Henrique on his right side, successfully adjusting my weight to keep from rolling off his back and falling to the mat.

If necessary, I pause for a moment to readjust the positioning of my chest against Henrique's back.

  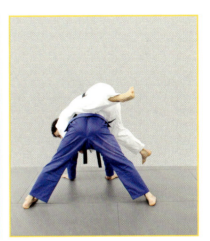

Using my seatbelt control as an anchor point, I swing myself to Henrique's back.

  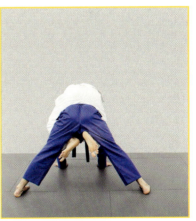

I weave my right foot over Henrique's right thigh and between his legs, curling my toes against the back of his right thigh to secure my first hook and to prevent myself from falling forward again. I repeat the same movement with my left leg to set my second hook.

SECURING THE FAR HOOK OPTION 1

Against an experienced competitor, taking the back will always be a challenge. Your opponent is afraid of giving up points, he is afraid of being submitted, and he wants to escape the position as soon as possible. When you establish the first hook, your opponent will realize that he is in danger of giving up his back, and he will panic, immediately defending the position in any way possible. One of the most common defenses you will encounter is a tight turtle that blocks the second hook. When this happens, roll your opponent onto his side and work to set your second hook from there. Though this movement has been a part of previous techniques, I am showing it to you in isolation so that I can cover the details of this crucial movement in greater depth.

Henrique is turtled. I have seatbelt control, and my right foot is already threaded between his legs, positioned as my first hook. In this scenario, his defense is too tight for me to transition directly to establishing my second hook.

I push off of the mat with my left foot to drive my weight forward and to collapse Henrique's right shoulder. I feel that his base is exceptionally strong, so I push off of the mat with the ball of my right foot for additional torque.

Continuing to drive off of the mat with my feet, I dip my right shoulder and use my tight seatbelt grip to pull Henrique over. I drag him on to his right side, and my right foot naturally becomes my first back hook.

To complete the back-take, I snake my left foot over Henrique's left thigh to set my second hook.

HELPFUL HINT

A quick way to take note of your favorite videos or share them with friends is to record the Video ID #. This is a unique number assigned to every video on MGInAction.com. When you are watching your chosen video, check the address bar for the last 3-4 numbers on the end of the link:

http://www.mginaction.com/VideoDetails.aspx?VideoId=1290

Just swap out the video ID at the end of the URL to easily navigate between clips.

MGInAction.com

SECURING THE FAR HOOK OPTION 2

When you are attacking the turtle and are working to secure your second hook, your opponent may prevent you from dragging him to his side by rolling away. By rolling away, your opponent can escape your back control and lock you in half guard or full guard. That is the best avenue for escape available to your opponent, so you should always be ready to counter it. If you react in time, you can roll with your opponent and set your second hook. Proper timing will obviously be a factor in your success, but your positioning is just as important. When you follow your opponent's roll, do not allow him to turn into you; remain attached to his upper back. Also, do not allow his hips to touch the mat. As he rolls away, position your knee between his hip and the mat to give yourself a leverage point for continuing the roll and setting your second hook.

Henrique is turtled, and I am controlling him with a seatbelt grip. My right foot is positioned as my first hook, and I am looking to establish my second hook.

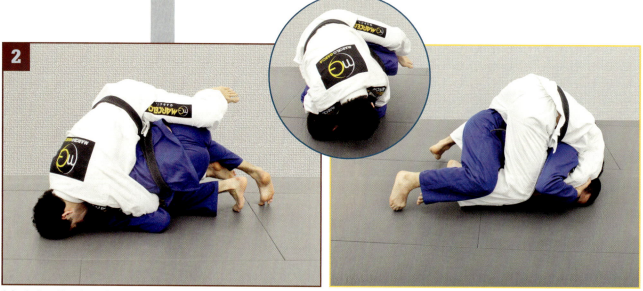

I feel that Henrique is tucking his left shoulder, beginning to collapse to his side to roll me into his guard. Before his left hip touches the mat, I swing my left leg over his back, moving faster than he is.

3

I shoot my left knee against Henrique's left hip.

4

As Henrique continues to roll, I follow him and use my seatbelt grip to guide his torso on top of my left knee. If I allow his hip to touch the mat, he could escape.

5

I drag Henrique's hips so that they are directly on top of mine and his chest is facing the ceiling. To give myself more leverage to manipulate his weight, I push off of the mat with my left foot.

I continue to roll Henrique to my right. I land on my right side, still securely attached to Henrique's back.

I maneuver my left foot over Henrique's left thigh to set my second hook. I can now work to finish the fight with a submission.

HIP EXTENSION

When you are fighting for your second hook, you may need to use a combination of techniques to ultimately secure the position that you want. The previous two techniques will get your opponent out of the turtle position and to his side, where securing the second hook is typically easier, but most grapplers will continue to defend from their side, blocking your second hook to improve their chances of escaping. One of the most common defenses you encounter is a knee and elbow frame, which is when your opponent connects his knee to his elbow to prevent you from setting your foot over his hip. Before you can improve your position and finish the fight, you must stretch your opponent out to open him up.

I am controlling Henrique with a seatbelt grip and am attempting to set my left foot in front of his left thigh to secure my second hook, but he is tucking his left knee against his chest and left elbow to block me.

I cross my ankles to lock my feet together and tuck my head against Henrique's left shoulder to eliminate any space between my chest and his back.

Pulling his back against my chest, I begin to bridge my hips into Henrique to stretch him out.

I arch my back and drive my hips forward until Henrique completely opens up. When performed properly, this movement is difficult to resist and even somewhat painful.

Moving quickly to set my hook before Henrique resumes his compact, defensive position, I uncross my ankles and swing my left foot around his left leg.

I set my left foot against Henrique's groin to secure back control.

COUNTER ROLL ESCAPE

Achieving and maintaining back control is a battle. You need a variety of weapons to acquire a dominant position and end the fight with a submission. In the previous technique, you used a hip extension to open a compact, defensive opponent to set your second hook. As you are battling for that second hook, your opponent could attempt to roll away from your first hook and escape. If you are aware of that possibility and anticipate your opponent's escape, you can counter with a variation of the hip extension to prevent him from switching sides. Again, your reaction time is a major factor in countering, so put in the hours to master the various techniques for maintaining the back position, and train yourself to use them in combination.

Henrique and I are on our right sides. I am controlling him with a seatbelt grip and my right hook is set. I am working to set my second hook, but he is blocking me with his left knee.

I lower my left foot, looking to use the hip extension to stretch out Henrique, but he is waiting for me to lower my left leg so that he can escape.

Henrique kicks off of his right foot and swings his left leg to his left in an effort to drive his left hip to the mat.

SECURING THE SECOND HOOK

Acting as soon as I feel Henrique begin to escape, I post my left foot on the mat behind me and bridge my hips into his lower back, pulling backward with my seatbelt control for additional leverage. If I execute this movement before he faces his chest to the sky, he will not be able to finish his roll.

While continuing to arch my back and bridge my hips, I drop Henrique back onto his right side by jerking on his chest with the seatbelt. As he falls, I am careful to keep my right foot laced around his right leg.

I then slide my left knee up Henrique's side and begin maneuvering my left foot over his left thigh.

I set my left foot on top of Henrique's left thigh, securing my second hook and establishing back control.

COUNTER BRIDGE ESCAPE

If your opponent faces his chest to the ceiling by rolling away from you or by bridging, you need to put him back on his side as soon as possible. If you hesitate to act, he could put his hip on the mat, trap your underhook between his ribs and the mat, and execute a high-percentage escape. When your opponent rests his weight directly on top of you, it is too late to use the hip extension. Using the foot on your underhook side, hook the back of your opponent's knee and lift his leg to guide him back to the mat. In the sequence below, I demonstrate this movement having only one hook set. Should you find yourself with both hooks and your opponent flattening your back to the mat as he switches sides, remove one of your hooks and execute the same counter. Countering your opponent's bridge escape is more important than having both hooks, and the more comfortable you become fighting with the seatbelt and just one hook, the more dangerous your back control game will become.

I am on Henrique's back. My seatbelt control is tight, and my right foot is set as my first hook. Remember, I would use this same counter even if I had both hooks.

Henrique digs his feet into the mat and begins to bridge to his left.

As Henrique faces his chest to the ceiling and my back to the mat, I circle my left foot under his left leg. If I had begun this counter with both hooks set, I would remove the hook on my underhook side, not my overhook side.

I hook the inside of Henrique's left knee with my left foot and begin to elevate his left leg.

I lift Henrique's left leg as high as I can with my left foot. The higher his leg, the longer my lever, which means that I will have more leverage.

MG IN ACTION

6

I guide Henrique's left leg to my right and turn him with my seatbelt grip, rotating his hips away from me to drop him on his right side.

7

Unhooking Henrique's left leg, I begin to circle my left foot in front of his left thigh.

COUNTER HIP ESCAPE

Whether I am controlling my opponent with one hook or two, losing my bottom hook can be disastrous. Without the bottom hook, I cannot prevent my opponent from hipping away and turning his back to the mat. In most cases, if my opponent reaches down to remove my hook with his hand, I can jam my arm into his neck and finish with him a rear naked choke, but if he is strong or agile, I may not be able to set the choke before he escapes. When I feel that the choke is not available, I make recovering the back position my main priority. If you glance at the sequence below, you will see that countering the hip escape requires a great deal of movement, but as long as your seatbelt is tight, completing the technique should not be difficult. As I have said before, the seatbelt is somewhat of an advanced concept, so do not be disheartened by the learning curve. I only use techniques that I feel are effective, and the techniques that I teach in this book are techniques that I use every day.

Henrique is on his right side, and I am on his back and have seatbelt control.

Henrique reaches for my right heel with his right hand, beginning a fundamental back-control escape. I attempt to choke him, but he is protecting his neck.

Henrique peels my right foot off of his hip and begins to hip over my right leg. He is now free of both hooks, and I need to counter his escape or he will reverse the position.

MG IN ACTION

I squeeze with my seatbelt grip to keep my chest as close to Henrique's upper back as possible while simultaneously shrimping my hips away from him.

I continue to shrimp and am wary of Henrique hooking one of my legs with his legs or his arms. If I let him grab one of my legs, he can prevent my counter and take the top position.

As I continue rotating behind Henrique, I begin to turn my hips to face the mat.

I am now directly behind Henrique, my chest still attached to his upper back.

8

Without loosening my seatbelt control, I crawl my right knee forward, driving my chest forward, bending Henrique's neck.

9

I crawl my knees forward to move my hips closer to Henrique's back and to come up onto my knees.

10

As I come up onto my knees, I press my chest to Henrique's shoulder blades to lift his back off of the mat. I walk my knees close to Henrique's back, eliminating the space between his back and my hips.

To set my hook on the overhook side, in this case my right side, I lean to the left slightly and swing my right foot around Henrique, planting it between his legs. Since I had to swivel my body slightly to place my right foot, my left leg is now folded behind him, the inside of my ankle facing his back.

I fall back and to my right side, using the seatbelt to drag Henrique with me. Having my left leg folded behind him makes this movement easy and comfortable for me.

I thread my left foot over Henrique's left thigh to establish my second hook, regaining back control.

COUNTER HIGH CROTCH TO BACK CONTROL

The reality of jiu-jitsu competition is that every match starts standing, and you will not always be the first to attack. If your opponent shoots for a takedown, you have an opportunity to sprawl and take his back. Though I advocate constant aggression, having to defend is inevitable, but never simply defend against an attack. Defend and counter at the same time to swing the momentum of the match back in your favor. In this technique, you sprawl and establish a front headlock to defend against a high crotch takedown. Once you have escaped his grips, you spin to his back.

Henrique and I are squared off, both hunting for takedowns.

Henrique lowers his hips, changing levels to initiate a takedown.

Henrique drives his right knee forward, planting it between my legs as he hooks my right leg and positions his head to the outside of my right hip.

4

Before Henrique can complete his takedown, I kick my legs backward, weakening his grip on my right leg. To prevent him from following me as I sprawl, I hook my right arm in front of his left shoulder and snake my left arm under his right armpit, grabbing my right wrist with my left hand.

5

To completely free my right leg, I extend my right leg farther back and sink my right hip to the mat.

6

With my right leg no longer in danger, I lift my right leg and swing it over my left leg, unlocking my arms and swiveling to my left, my chest pressing against his back, acting as a rotation point.

7

I plant my right foot behind me, resting the majority of my weight on Henrique's back. I then wrap my right arm around his right shoulder and my left arm under his left armpit to begin securing the seatbelt.

8

I scissor my legs, sliding my right leg under my left to rotate my hips, facing them down toward the mat. I use the position change to tighten my seatbelt control.

9

With a tight seatbelt established, I push off of the mat with my toes, driving my body into Henrique.

mG IN ACTION

10

I kick off of the mat, elevating my hips.

11

I jam my right knee under Henrique's right hip as I use the momentum of my jump to drag him onto his right side.

12

I plant my right foot on the mat and point my right knee to the ceiling, rotating his chest upward. If I allow his right hip to touch the mat, he could shrimp out and escape. By using my knee to reposition his hips in this step, I create enough space to secure my first hook.

Using the space I created in the previous step, I flick my right foot in front of Henrique's right thigh as I drop him back onto his right side. With my first hook set, I immediately lift my left foot into the air to begin securing my second hook.

I set my left foot in front of Henrique's left thigh, scoring me four points.

HELPFUL HINT

MGInAction.com is a very flexible site when it comes to finding related techniques. Our comprehensive tagging system allows you to move fluidly between progressions in movement, by giving you 'Research Suggestions' and 'Related Techniques and Instructionals'. Just look on the right side of the page when you are looking at videos to see what the program will suggest for you.

MGInAction.com

COUNTER SITTING SINGLE-LEG TO BACK CONTROL OPTION 1

Whenever you are working from the sprawl, no matter what takedown your opponent uses, you have the chance to take his back if you can break his grip and clear his arms. In many cases, however, trying to transition from a sprawl into any sort of attack creates a scramble. Your opponent knows that his takedown attempt has failed, and he does not want to be caught in a bad position or worse, a submission. When this happens, many grapplers will go to their guard, which forces you to start working to pass. If your opponent sits up and you are able to stand, you can bait him into attacking your leg so that you can take his back. As you work through the sequence below, remember that this particular back-take hinges upon positioning your opponent's head to the outside of your leg. If his head is on the inside, this technique will not work. In that situation, use the subsequent move instead.

Henrique is in a seated guard, and I am standing, looking to pass.

I shoot my hands forward and grab Henrique's ankles.

As I straighten my back, I lift Henrique's ankles, forcing him to rock onto his back.

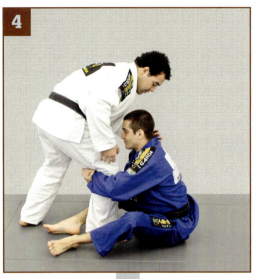

As I step forward with my right foot, I release Henrique's ankles. He rocks forward, back to a seated guard, and wraps his arms around my legs. When I see that he is taking the bait and attacking with a single-leg, I cup the right side of his head as he sits up and begin to guide it to my right, outside of my right leg.

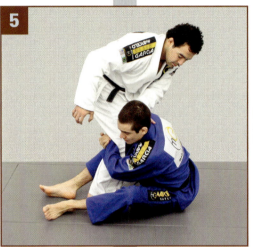

I shove Henrique's head to the outside of my right thigh and step my left forward at the same time.

Pivoting on my right foot, I swing my left leg behind Henrique and drop my chest onto his shoulders, lacing my right arm between his head and right shoulder as I lower my upper body.

I plant my left foot against the small of Henrique's back and lock the seatbelt.

Dropping my left knee to the mat, facing the inside of my left ankle and left knee to Henrique's back, I squeeze my chest to his back and sit back to my right to drag Henrique on to his right side.

As soon as we land on our sides, I slide my left thigh up Henrique's side.

I lift my left leg, looking to set my second hook. I hook the inside of Henrique's left thigh to establish back control.

COUNTER SITTING SINGLE-LEG TO BACK CONTROL OPTION 2

In the previous technique, my opponent attempted a single-leg from the seated guard, and I guided his head to the outside to set up a back-take. Unfortunately, not all opponents will fall for my trap. If an opponent manages to get his head inside of my thigh when he attempts the single-leg, I am somewhat vulnerable to being taken down. I need to first free my leg to prevent the takedown, and then I can capitalize on his scramble to step to his back. When you feel that your opponent is clinging desperately to the single-leg, you should be confident that he is committed to moving forward and will expose his back in the process. This movement seems fancy, but it is quite practical and relatively easy to execute after a bit of practice.

Henrique is in the seated guard position and I am standing, looking for an opening to pass or to bait him into giving me his back.

I shoot my arms forward and latch on to Henrique's ankles.

Lifting Henrique's legs into the air, I force him to rock onto his back.

Henrique fights to regain the seated guard by posting on his hands and crunching his chest forward even though I am still holding his ankles.

I drop Henrique's ankles and step my right foot forward between his legs. He sits up and takes the bait, wrapping his left arm around my right leg to initiate a single-leg takedown. I would have liked to use the previous technique to take his back, but Henrique is smart and refuses to allow me to push his head to the outside of my right thigh.

Turning my hips and knees away from Henrique, I plant my right hand on the left side of his face and press his head toward the mat. At the same time, I lift my right leg and begin to yank it free of his clutches.

I kick my right leg free of Henrique's grasp and do not yet release his head until my leg is completely free. Sometimes, I may need to jerk my right leg repeatedly to escape his grip.

Henrique is slow to react to my freeing my leg and lingers in the seated guard position, leaning forward. I capitalize on the position by lifting my right leg and swinging it over his head toward his back. I plant my right foot on the mat directly behind Henrique, straddling him.

I collapse my weight onto Henrique, pressing my chest into his upper back. At the same time, I slide my left arm over his left shoulder and down his chest, and I thread my right arm under his right armpit. My hands meet in the middle and secure a seatbelt grip. As I fight for my seatbelt control with my hands, I begin to sit back by straightening my left leg and keeping my right foot posted while bending my right knee.

10

As I lower my hips to the mat, I twist to my left, dragging Henrique with me. When my butt hits the ground, I press my right knee against Henrique's right side and continue to twist to my left.

11

I land on my left side with my left hook set and my chest squeezed tightly to Henrique's upper back.

12

I maneuver my right foot over Henrique's right thigh to secure back control.

COUNTER SITTING SINGLE-LEG OPTION 3

Freeing your leg from a head-inside single is not always as easy as yanking your leg out. Against a talented wrestler or in the gi where there is a great deal of friction, your leg is likely to get stuck, requiring more effort and multiple jerks to pull the leg away. When this happens, your opponent will follow you, clinging to your leg and transitioning to his knees. Even when you escape your leg, your opponent will not give up. He will use the momentum of your escape to continue coming forward, sometimes reaching to grab your other leg. Rather than continue to scramble, I prefer to take the back, but to do that, I must commit to kicking my leg free. If my kick is weak, my opponent will take me down.

Henrique is attacking my right leg with a head-inside single, and his grip is exceptionally tight.

I plant my right hand on the back of Henrique's neck and press downward as I turn my hips and knees away.

3

I attempt to yank my leg free, but Henrique maintains his grip and comes up onto his knees to increase his leverage.

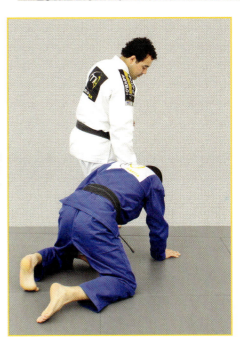

4

Continuing to post my right hand on the back of Henrique's neck to delay him from moving forward, I kick my right leg forward as hard as I can as though I am punting a soccer ball.

5

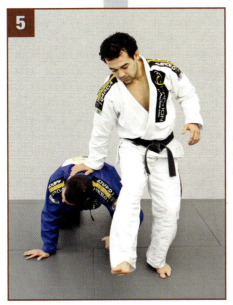

The strength of my kick is too great for Henrique to resist. My right leg slips free of his grasp.

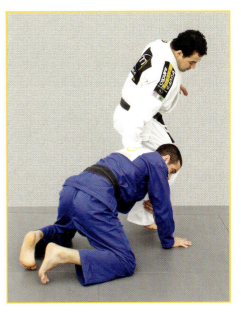

COUNTER TACTICS

Henrique naturally continues to move forward, either carried by the momentum of my kick or because he intends to attack my left leg. In either case, I swing my right leg up and over his head

As my right leg falls to the mat, I drop my chest to Henrique's back and secure a seatbelt by looping my right arm under his right armpit and my left arm over his left shoulder.

Before Henrique can establish a tight turtle position, I squeeze my chest to his back and throw myself to my left to drag him onto his left side. If he does turtle, I will use one of the techniques for securing the second hook that I taught earlier.

MG IN ACTION

9

I land on my left side with my left foot in place as my first hook.

10

To earn four points, I snake my right foot over Henrique's right hip, establishing my second hook.

MG FAST FACT

Taking the back as a counter to the low single leg is one of Marcelo's primary defensive moves from this position. As Marcelo's opponents commit to the single leg, they will often have their heads up, leaving their necks open for a high percentage finish with a choke from the back.

For an efficient way to study the content, go to the 'InAction' tab and click on 'Load to Queue'.

MGInAction.com

COUNTER KNEE-ON-BELLY ESCAPE

Any time your opponent turns his back toward the ceiling—not necessarily because of a failed shot—you have the chance to take his back. Many of these opportunities arise when your opponent attempts to escape from the bottom. He knows that he gives up points by letting you pass his guard, and he knows that he needs to escape to avoid being submitted. When you have the knee-on-belly position, your opponent is especially prone to overcommitting to an escape because the pressure of the position is immense and often painful. As your opponent turns in and comes to his knees, spin to the opposite side and take his back. The mechanics of this counter are very similar to the single-leg counter that you learned earlier because your opponent is initiating a single-leg as he escapes knee-on-belly. Though the starting point may be different, the middle and ending points are not. With practice, you will begin to see the commonalities between seemingly different positions, and you will see that a few common principles can be applied in many situations.

I have my right knee on Henrique's stomach, maintaining the knee-on-belly position to create enough discomfort to force him to react.

Henrique bridges and turns toward me, swimming his left arm around my right thigh.

3

As Henrique transitions to his knees to initiate a single-leg takedown, I sprawl my legs back to weaken his grip on my right leg and to prevent him from locking his hands together.

4

Moving on the balls of my feet, I circle to my left, toward Henrique's head, swinging my right arm to the left side of his body as I turn.

5

As I pivot parallel to Henrique, I angle my left hip toward the mat and kick my right leg behind me, stepping over my left leg.

6

I plant my right foot on the mat behind me, achieving a position similar to a sit-out. To break any remaining grip that he might have, I sink my hips to the mat.

7

To begin securing my seatbelt, I swing my left leg under my right, turning my chest toward the mat.

8

Balancing on my toes, I press my chest into Henrique's upper back and punch my right arm in front of his right shoulder, grabbing my right wrist with my left hand to lock the seatbelt.

In one motion, I jump into the air, swinging my left leg over Henrique's lower back as I jam my right knee into the small gap between Henrique's right triceps and the top of his right thigh.

Without loosening my seatbelt grip, I fall to my right side, dragging Henrique with me. As I fall, I elevate his hips with my right knee.

Before Henrique's hips hit the mat, I swim my right foot in front of Henrique's right thigh.

To establish back mount, I swing my left leg over Henrique's left hip.

COUNTER SIDE CONTROL UNDERHOOK ESCAPE

Countering an underhook side control escape with a back-take is similar to countering a knee-on-belly escape. Just like the previous technique, you capitalize on his need to escape, sprawl to weaken his single-leg attempt, and switch to the opposite side with a big step backward. In the context of a match, transitioning to the back likely will not be your first option when you have side control, but if you fail to sink the far underhook and your opponent instead establishes his underhook, this is a great technique to turn what would usually be a bad situation for you into a shortcut to the back. If you ever feel yourself losing side control, use this technique immediately to stay on top and to protect your positioning.

I have Henrique in side control, and I failed to thread my right arm under his armpit to establish my underhook.

Henrique begins to slip his left hand under my right armpit.

3

Henrique shoots his left arm into a deep underhook and bridges into me to begin turning to his knees.

4

As Henrique fights to transition to his knees, I extend my right leg to weaken any grip that he may have been able to establish.

5

As I kick my right leg behind me and over my left leg, I circle toward Henrique's head.

I plant my right foot on the mat to Henrique's right. Though he has scrambled to his knees, my legs are free, and by switching to the opposite side I have opened a path to his back.

I turn my chest to Henrique's back swinging my left leg under my right leg.

I glue my chest to Henrique's shoulders blades as I lock the seatbelt, overhooking his right shoulder and underhooking his left arm.

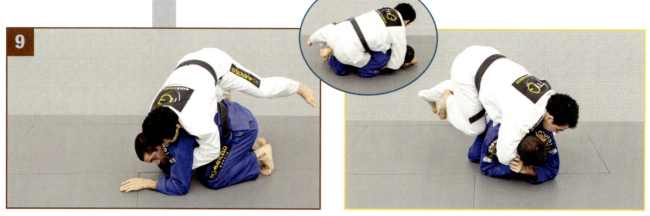

To drag Henrique onto his side, I jump my right knee into his ribs, my right shin resting on the middle of his right thigh.

As I drag Henrique's weight on top of me, I flare my right knee toward the ceiling to create space between his side and the mat.

I snake my right foot out from beneath Henrique using the space I created in the previous step and set it on his right thigh, securing my first hook.

I maneuver my left foot over Henrique's left thigh, setting my second hook and securing back control.

COUNTER TACTICS

COUNTER SIDE CONTROL RUN ESCAPE

Your opponent will use a variety of techniques to escape side control. Using an underhook to get to his knees is probably the most common, but when that fails, many grapplers will turn away, confident that they can reach a secure turtle position despite having to show their back to get there. If you do not know the secrets of the seatbelt, your opponent could very well succeed. Very few people see the opening to establish seatbelt control in this scenario, but once you learn this technique, your opponent's attempt to turn away from you will not be an escape. It will be a mistake, and you will take his back. Remember, the principles of the seatbelt remain constant regardless of how you set it up. In this position, even though your opponent's back is low, you must still attach your chest to the center of his upper back to lock a strong, secure seatbelt. Never compromise and accept an inferior grip. Always achieve the most technical grip possible.

I have Henrique in side control.

Henrique's posture is strong, and I am unable to find an opening for an attack, so I lift my chest and grab his right wrist with my left hand, baiting him to turn away from me. If I do not control his right arm in some manner, he will most likely turn into me and use it to establish an underhook.

Henrique takes the bait and begins to turn away from me. I immediately drop my chest low to the mat, aiming to plant my chest against his upper back as he turns.

As Henrique continues to turn away, I follow him, attaching my chest to his upper back. At the same time, I loop my left arm under his left arm and thread my right arm over his right shoulder.

I grab my right wrist with my left hand, locking the seatbelt. I sink my hips and squeeze with my arms to stall Henrique on his side. I could take his back as he turtles, but taking his back when he is on his side will actually be easier.

Without loosening the seatbelt, I tuck my right knee against Henrique's right shoulder blade.

7

Balancing my weight on my right knee and on Henrique's back, I lift my left leg, swinging it over his hips.

8

I plant my left foot against Henrique's right hip.

9

I fold my right leg underneath my hips, aligning my right shin with Henrique's spine, and sit back, using the seatbelt to drag him with him.

10

As I sit back, I twist to my left, centering Henrique between my legs as I escape my right foot. I could fall to my left side and set my second hook from there, but I do not want to fight from my underhook side, so I opt to set my second hook while we are both sitting up.

I set my right foot against the inside of Henrique's right thigh, securing my second hook.

With both hooks set, I fall to my right, pulling Henrique with me. Now that I am fighting from my overhook side, I am in a great position to finish the fight.

HELPFUL HINT

On MGInAction.com, we've organized all the various techniques into positional tree that is located in your 'Training Database'. Begin by clicking on the origin of your position, for ex: 'Side Control'. Once you decide on your position, you can further narrow your search by intention, for ex: 'Controls and Grips', 'Submissions', 'Escapes', 'Transitions', 'Submission Escapes'. You can then find more specific videos based on your criteria. Using this tool, you can find a variety of ways in which you can learn and identify with the position within the context of Marcelo's Game.

If you can't find what you're looking for using the tree, try searching for videos using other details that you like about the technique. For example, if you're looking for techniques on taking the back, you can start here:
Back / Transitions / Taking the Back
If you're not satisfied with your results, try searching with a new detail, like 'taking the back from the guard':
Guard / Butterfly / Transitions / 2 on 1 Butterfly to Back
For an efficient way to study the content, go to the 'InAction' tab and click on 'Load to Queue'.

MGInAction.com

BUTTERFLY GUARD SWEEP TO BACK CONTROL

In this chapter, I have covered a variety of counters that end with a back-take. We have addressed countering takedowns and countering escapes, but if at any point I can trick my opponent into showing his back, I can potentially establish seatbelt control, set my hooks, and secure the back position. Such opportunities will not necessarily arise in positions where you would conventionally think of taking the back. For example, if I use the arm drag to set up a butterfly sweep, I can threaten a sweep to bait my opponent into letting me take his back (for a more extensive breakdown of my butterfly guard, check out my previous book, The X-Guard). This technique may seem out of place given the other counters I have covered, but I want you to see the extent of my aggressiveness. I am never content with a simple sweep if I can take the back instead, and I look to take the back from every position. You will notice that this technique employs the grip fighting principles that we covered in the first chapter. Even though I am beginning this technique with a butterfly sweep, the control that the arm drag position provides—and keep in mind that the gi and no-gi variations are interchangeable—is versatile. I can use it to set up an arm drag or a butterfly sweep, or a combination of both.

I start the technique from the seated guard with Henrique looking to pass from his knees.

I latch on to Henrique's right wrist with my left hand.

I reach across with my right hand and grip the far side of Henrique's right sleeve, securing a pistol grip. I position my right hand to the outside of his right wrist and lock my arm in place. If I allow his right hand to pummel inside of my right arm, he can grab my collar.

MG IN ACTION

I clamp on to Henrique's right elbow with my left hand and drag it to my right, forcing his torso to twist away from me somewhat.

While using my grips to keep Henrique turned to his left, I extend my legs, setting my feet between his legs and digging my heels into the mat.

I scoot my hips forward, closing the distance between Henrique and me to establish butterfly guard. Notice that his right arm is still positioned across his body.

7

I rock backward, using the arm drag position to pull Henrique forward.

8

As Henrique's weight shifts forward, I lift my feet to elevate his hips, balancing the entirety of his body over my legs and hips.

9

I kick my right foot to the sky, throwing Henrique's left leg higher than his right, which forces his hips to rotate.

I yank Henrique's right arm to my right with my right hand to turn his back to my chest as he falls between my legs. It's important to note that my left hand releases his right elbow in this step.

Henrique lands on his right side, and I settle my right leg against the inside of his right thigh, securing my first hook. I underhook his left arm with my left to begin establishing the seatbelt.

I maneuver my left leg over Henrique's left hip to get my four points.

SUBMISSIONS FROM BACK CONTROL

My submission game from the back, at its core, is incredibly simple. I want the rear naked choke. I know it. My opponent knows it. Anyone that has watched me compete in the last decade knows it. I may deviate from this game plan and transition to another submission if I am absolutely sure that I can finish it, but typically if I take the back, I am determined to win by rear naked choke.

I have been asked on numerous occasions by a multitude of grapplers, "What is your secret? What is the trick to getting the rear naked choke? How did you develop the power of your choke?" The truth is that there is no magic secret to being successful with the rear naked choke. No sleight of hand or ancient ki technique. Jiu-jitsu is not a mystical art. There are no hidden moves. You already know why I have been so successful with the rear naked choke. It is the same reason any grappler is good with any submission: practice. Many fighters specialize in the guard position, but unlike the back position, the guard is relatively simple to achieve. A grappler can touch hands and immediately start working from his guard, both in the gym and in competition. That makes packing on the practice hours in that position easy. If you have been training for a few years, consider how much time you have spent in the guard versus having back control. The difference in hours is likely to be monumental.

You have dedicated a significant portion of your training to perfecting how you retain the guard, how you set up your favorite submissions and sweeps from the guard, and the timing with which you execute those techniques. Your triangle used to lead to you getting passed, but now the fight is over if you can clear one of your opponent's arms and secure the position. Your legs used to gas out when you tried to hold closed guard, but now your strength and endurance has developed to the point that you can hold the closed guard indefinitely. A simple pass used to blast right through your defenses, but now you can counter a variety of passes and even use those pass attempts to set up a sweep or a submission.

Compare that to how you attack from the back. You struggle to get to the back position consistently. When you do take the back, you can only maintain the position for a few moments before your opponent escapes. Your seatbelt control gases out your arms. You lose the grip battle. When you do attempt the rear naked choke, you cannot break through your opponent's resistance or set your arms properly. This situation is analogous to the hardships you faced with your guard.

My rear naked choke is effective because I have practiced it over and over for hours and hours against a variety of training partners and opponents. Do not forget that I have been training three to five times a day since I was a teenager. Admittedly, my training schedule allowed me to accumulate practice

hours quickly, but I still put the hours in. You have to do the same thing. There is no shortcut. Once you can execute your back attacks flawlessly against a nonresisting opponent, you have to put your time in against resisting opponents. That is assuming that you have developed your ability to take the back to the point that you can do it consistently. With practice, your timing will improve. The strength of your squeeze will increase. And the rear naked choke will become one of your best submissions.

SUBMISSION BEFORE POSITION

Conventional jiu-jitsu wisdom says to only attack with a submission once you have established control in a dominant position. I agree with this philosophy for the most part, but in my mind, there is one key exception: the rear naked choke from the back. If I can sink the rear naked choke, I will, regardless of whether or not I have one hook, two hooks, or no hooks at all. When my opponent exposes his neck, I will skip directly to the choke because I am confident in the power of my choke, and I know that I may not have another opportunity to finish the fight before time expires. With nearly every grappler subscribing to the "position before submission" mantra, using the rear naked choke before I have established back control often surprises my opponents. They assume that I will not look for a submission before I have my hooks set.

My hyperaggressive approach to the rear naked choke helped me to win the 2003 ADCC. My match with Vitor "Shaolin" Ribeiro had just begun, and after a successful arm drag, I was on Shaolin's back. But Shaolin was talented and incredibly fast. He immediately attempted to roll out of my back control, but I stayed with him. For a brief instant, I had one hook set, but Shaolin was so focused on escaping the position that he neglected to protect his neck. I secured the rear naked choke and stuck to Shaolin's back as he thrashed like a hooked fish. He rolled and rolled and then he stopped. The referee was confused. He prodded Shaolin's limp body and then frantically pulled me off. Shaolin was unconscious. Had I waited to secure my hooks, I may have never had the opportunity to set the choke and could have fought Shaolin for the rest of the match. Instead, my rear naked choke finished the fight in twenty-two seconds. My combination of aggression and technique paid off in a big way.

ANATOMY OF A REAR NAKED CHOKE

As I mentioned in the introduction to this chapter, I attribute much of my success with the rear naked choke to my high level of aggressiveness. If my opponent's neck is open, I attack it, regardless of my position. I may have two hooks in, one hook in, or no hooks at all. If I can close the choke, I go for it because I am confident that my squeeze will put my opponent to sleep before he can find a way to escape. Developing a strong rear naked choke, like anything else, takes practice, but keep these two concepts in mind:

1) I do not slide my choking arm from shoulder to shoulder to slip it under the neck. Instead, I pop my choking arm straight up from seatbelt control, jamming it into his neck. This approach is faster than the traditional movement for setting the choking arm, and since it is somewhat more violent, the choke sets a bit deeper, increasing the pressure of my squeeze

2) When I squeeze the choke, I am not just flexing my arms. I pinch my elbows together, chop the hand that is behind his neck downward, and arch my back to stretch my opponent out, driving the choke deeper as I pull him into me.

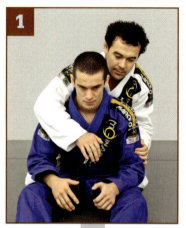

I am on Henrique's back and see that his neck is exposed.

I jam the blade of my right wrist under his chin and into his neck. This is not a slow movement. It is quick and violent so that I can capitalize on what is usually a small and very brief opening.

I dig my fingers of my right hand into the groove of his left shoulder blade to momentarily stabilize the position and align his chin with the bend of my right elbow. If I need to, I can walk my fingers across his shoulder to reach this position.

Without relaxing the pressure of my right arm against Henrique's neck, I point my left hand to the ceiling and raise my arm.

As I hop my right hand onto my left biceps, I bend my left wrist to fold my left hand toward my chest.

I thread my left arm behind Henrique's neck, facing my left palm to my chest. To finish the fight, I squeeze my elbows together, chop my left hand downward, and pull his neck toward me with both arms.

SQUEEZE DETAIL

In the first photograph, the gap where my opponent's neck would be is large. To begin closing the gap, I chop my left hand downward. In the final photograph, you can see that I am squeezing my elbows together to eliminate the last bit of space, but notice the difference in the positioning of my right hand between the second and third photograph. In the third photograph, I am reaching as far beyond my left biceps as I can to tighten my squeeze.

ALTERNATE BACK CHOKE

The rear naked choke is the ideal submission from the back, but setting and finishing it is always a challenge. If am able to jam my wrist into my opponent's neck but he prevents me from grabbing my biceps to lock the rear naked choke, I transition to this alternate finishing grip to end the fight. Tucking my arm under his chin is an opportunity that I cannot waste, and I am content to choke my opponent in any way possible. When you apply this choke, be on the lookout for an opening to lock in the rear naked choke. Threatening one choke will often lead to the other, so be prepared to switch between the two if necessary.

I am on Henrique's back, looking for the rear naked choke.

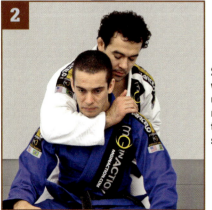

Seeing that his neck is exposed, I wedge the blade of my right wrist under his neck. I attempt to slide my right arm across his neck to set the rear naked choke, but he is resisting.

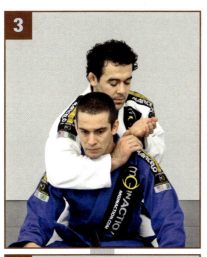

I transition to an alternate back choke by setting the back of my left hand on Henrique's left shoulder.

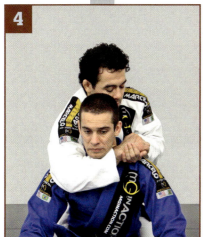

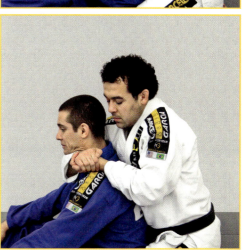

I clasp my hands together.

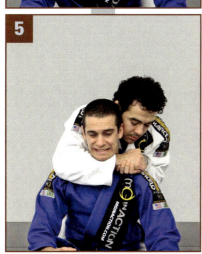

To finish the choke, I set my left forearm against Henrique's spine and squeeze my arms as I pull back. If I need to, I can tighten the choke by walking my hands up his shoulder like I was tightening a bolt with a ratchet.

OVERHOOK ARM TRAP TO REAR CHOKE

As soon as you take your opponent's back, his first reaction will be to protect his neck. Grapplers develop this instinct early in their careers, and after years and years of being attacked with the rear naked choke, most are very adept at defending against it. They tuck their chins, and they latch on to your arms with a death grip, preventing you from getting to their neck. And they rarely focus entirely on blocking the choke. They block the choke and attempt to escape your back control, trying to roll away, to shuck off your hooks, and to put you on your back. Since your opponent is well-aware that he is in danger and that you want to sink the rear naked choke, you will likely need to break his defenses down before you can set your choking arm. Trapping one of his arms with your legs is a great way to create an opening for the choke, especially if you can trap the hand that will give you the most trouble: the hand on your overhook side. Also included in this sequence is a strategy for sinking your choking arm even deeper, so pay close attention to the details contained within the captions.

I am on Henrique's back with a seatbelt grip established. He is desperately protecting his neck.

As I retract my right arm, I grab Henrique's left lapel with my left hand.

I latch on to Henrique's right wrist with my right hand and do not release his lapel.

I punch my right hand downward, rotating the inside of my elbow to face his chest to achieve the optimal amount of leverage from the movement.

As I release Henrique's right wrist, I swing my right leg out and over his right arm. Notice that I have not released his lapel. By controlling his lapel throughout the technique I am more likely to maintain the back position.

To trap Henrique's right arm, I dig my right heel into his stomach, pinching his right arm against his body. For the arm trap to be successful, I set my leg as high on his arm as possible and slide down to trap it.

7

I release Henrique's left lapel and grab his left wrist with my left hand, pressing it away from his neck as I set the outside of my right thumb against his neck.

8

To begin setting the rear naked choke, I slide my right thumb up Henrique's chest until it comes into contact with his chin.

9

While digging my thumb into Henrique's chin, I rotate my right wrist upward to lift his chin and expose his neck. If necessary, I will do this repeatedly.

10

Once he is vulnerable, I shoot my right arm across his neck and grab his left shoulder.

I flare my right elbow to the sky to further expose Henrique's neck.

I punch my right arm across Henrique's neck, sinking a deep choke as I align the bend of my right elbow with his chin and dig my fingers into the groove of his left shoulder.

I grab my left biceps with my right hand and fold my left arm behind Henrique's head, locking the rear naked choke.

To finish the fight, I drag Henrique on to his right side and apply finishing pressure.

UNDERHOOK ARM TRAP TO REAR CHOKE

If I need to trap one of my opponent's arms, I always prefer to trap the arm on my overhook side, since that arm is in a stronger defensive position than the other arm, and I can fall to that side to use my opponent's weight to keep his arm trapped. However, most grapplers will control my overhook instinctively, and an athletic grappler will have a strong grip, sometimes too strong for me to break, and sometimes I will already be lying on my side, unable to escape my leg to trap his arm. If I can't stuff the arm on my overhook side, I attack the arm on my underhook side. Trapping either arm will mean he has one less hand with which to defend the choke, which is a significant advantage to have when fighting for the rear naked choke.

I have Henrique in back control, and he is gripping my right arm, preventing me from getting the choke. Normally I would attempt to use my overhook arm to set up an arm trap, but we are lying on our right sides, so I am unable to free my right leg.

I attack with my underhook arm instead. I thread my left hand on top of Henrique's left wrist, pressing it toward his hips as I rotate my left elbow, pointing it away from me to give me more power to stuff his arm.

As I continue to shove Henrique's left hand to his hip, I release my left hook and swing it out and up.

I hook my left leg over Henrique's left biceps and press my heel into his ribs to trap his left arm.

I yank my left arm out, freeing my left hand to begin attacking.

To clear a path for my choking arm, I grab Henrique's right hand with my left hand.

I peel Henrique's right hand off of my right wrist and force it toward my left ankle.

I jam my right arm into Henrique's neck to begin setting the rear naked choke. If he is tucking his chin, I can grind my wrist into position and then flare my elbow upward to force him to lift his head and expose his neck. For a refresher on that sequence, see the previous technique.

I grab my left biceps with my right hand and finish the rear naked choke.

BEHIND-THE-BACK ARM TRAP TO REAR CHOKE

Working to trap one of my opponent's arms with my legs is a great way to set up the rear naked choke because he will have one less tool with which to defend. I do not, however, always need to force the arm trap using the previous two techniques. An opponent may sometimes choose to expose his arm to attempt a back control escape—typically by reaching to attack my hooks. I can then use this lapse in my opponent's posture to control his vulnerable arm. I could simply trap his arm with my leg like I did before, but if my opponent is determined to remove one of my hooks, I can trick him into moving his arm behind his back, allowing me to trap it in a kimura-like position.

1

I have Henrique's back, and I am lying on my overhook side looking to finish the fight with a rear naked choke.

2

Henrique reaches down with his left hand and cups my left heel.

3

Henrique uses his left hand to pop my left hook off of his thigh, but I wait to counter.

4

When I see that Henrique has overcommitted to his escape, swinging his left arm past his hip and behind his back to remove my left hook, I shoot my left hand under his left arm and latch on to his wrist

As soon as I grab Henrique's left wrist with my left hand, I pull his left arm back, bending it like a kimura. At the same time, I kick my left leg straight to break his grip.

I plant Henrique's left hand into the middle of his upper back, wrenching his arm into a position where it is both weak and uncomfortable.

I drag my left knee up Henrique's ribs and wedge it into his left armpit. To stabilize this position, I dig my left foot into his left hip.

I cup Henrique's left shoulder with my left hand to maintain my position as I circle my right hand down and to the outside of his right wrist.

9

I latch on to Henrique's right wrist with my right hand.

10

Using the power of my right arm, I shove Henrique's right arm toward his waist and away from his neck. I release my grip on Henrique's left shoulder and set my left hand on his forehead.

11

I pull on Henrique's forehead with my left hand to peel his chin back, exposing his neck.

12

I shoot my right arm up Henrique's chest, jamming it into his throat.

13

Gripping my left biceps with my right hand, I slip my left hand behind Henrique's head and grip my right shoulder, squeezing my elbows together and arching my back to get the tap.

BOW AND ARROW CHOKE

While the rear naked choke is always my first option because of its simplicity and its finishing power, attacking with the rear naked choke will often distract my opponent from defending his lapels. If I can set a deep lapel grip with my top hand, I will use it to go for the submission. When I am competing in the gi, I have a variety of lapel attacks at my disposal, but the bow and arrow choke is one of my favorites because it is reliable, controlled, and powerful. Typically, I am hesitant to leave the back control position to attempt a submission because I do not want to risk sacrificing a dominant position, which is why I am not teaching you to attack with submissions like armbars from the back. The bow and arrow choke is an exception to this rule because it is methodical. If I begin to feel that I am not going to be able to finish the submission, I can usually return to back control with little difficulty.

I have Henrique's back, and I am fighting to sink the rear naked choke.

Distracted by having to defend his neck, Henrique forgets to defend his collar. I grab his left lapel with my left hand and pull it away from his chest.

3

I grab Henrique's left lapel with my right hand, clenching my fist to secure a tight hold. I grip it low because I assume that he will be protecting his neck.

4

As I slide my right hand up Henrique's left lapel, he tucks his chin to protect his neck.

5

I yank my left hand out from under Henrique's left arm.

6

I set my left hand on Henrique's forehead.

I crank Henrique's head back with my left hand and cinch his left collar around his neck. The benefit of the bow and arrow choke in this position is that I only need a sliver of space to slide his lapel against his neck, rather than the few inches that I would need for my wrist.

I remove my right hook and begin to turn to my left.

I kick my right leg out to turn myself perpendicular to Henrique, which begins to tighten the choke. As I do that, I reach my left arm under his left knee to hook his left leg. If his knee is out of reach, I will grab his pants, yank his left leg toward me, and jump my left arm into a leg hook. I do not want to finish the choke with a pants grip because he could easily kick free.

To finish the choke, I row my arms toward my ribs and extend my left leg. The pressure on Henrique's neck is immense, and his back will feel pain as well. It is important that I do not lift my right elbow in this step. I keep it clamped down to prevent him from slipping his head free.

GRIP FIGHTING TO THE BOW AND ARROW CHOKE

Tightening the bow and arrow choke against a stubborn opponent can quickly burn out your hands and weaken your grips. You should always expect your opponent to defend until the bitter end, so it is important to have an answer for every obstacle that he will put between you and your victory. In this technique, your opponent is desperately protecting his collar, and you use multiple grip breaks to cinch your lapel grip tighter and tighter. The key to these grip breaks is to begin peeling your opponent's hand at his thumb and end at his pinky, almost as though you were opening the lid on a piece of Tupperware.

I am on Henrique's back, working to finish the bow and arrow choke. I am gripping his left lapel with my right hand, but he is blocking me from sliding my right hand up to his neck by grabbing his own lapel with his left hand.

Without releasing my right hand, I thread my left hand under Henrique's left armpit, reaching for his left hand. I grab Henrique's left hand with my left hand, positioning his left thumb in the palm of my hand.

I peel Henrique's left hand off of his lapel by twisting my left hand forward as though I am throttling a motorcycle, releasing his thumb and pointer finger first, rotating the back of his hand down toward the mat.

I slide my right hand up Henrique's lapel, but before I can get to his neck he grabs his lapel again.

Since there is not a large enough gap for me to thread my left arm under his left arm, I reach over his left shoulder and latch on to his left hand.

I repeat the same grip peel that I used previously, ripping his left hand off of his lapel. I cinch my right hand as deep as I can. If I need to, I can grab his forehead to lift his chin before finishing the bow and arrow.

BOW AND ARROW ESCAPE COUNTER

If your opponent fails to protect his collar, his last line of defense is to run from your leg hook. To counter his escape, follow him with your leg and transition to technical mount as he attempts to belly down. Once you achieve technical mount, your opponent can no longer run, and his leg is again within reach. Technical mount is a powerful position that provides multiple options for submissions and transitions, but if you have already set the lapel grip, transition back to the bow and arrow choke as soon as you can to end the fight.

The bow and arrow choke finish is just a few movements away. I am gripping Henrique's left lapel with my right hand, and I am falling back to hook his left leg with my left hand.

As I reach to hook Henrique's left leg, he straightens his right leg and drapes his right arm over my right leg. He begins to turn to his right, away from the choke.

Henrique hops his hips over my right leg and runs to his right. Seeing that his left leg is now out of reach, I hug my chest to his back and follow him, hooking his right hip with my left foot.

Henrique turns on to his side as I throw my left arm forward, planting my left foot on the mat next to his hip as I sit up.

Since my right hand is still controlling Henrique's left lapel, I immediately transition back into the bow and arrow choke by leaning to my left, reaching to hook his left leg.

I hook the bend of Henrique's left knee with my left arm. It's important to note that I have not yet sat back. I am still leaning to my left.

With Henrique's left leg controlled, I begin to rock backward.

I finish the bow and arrow choke by rowing both of my elbows to my hips and extending my left leg.

COUNTER BACK ESCAPE TO BELLY-DOWN REAR CHOKE

When you are attacking from the back—whether going directly for the rear naked choke, trapping one of his arms with your legs, or transitioning to a collar choke—your opponent will always try to escape. We covered a number of counters for common escapes in the previous chapter, but each of those counters focused on regaining your position, not transitioning to a submission. I have mentioned multiple times that I will go directly for the choke if the opportunity presents itself, regardless of what position I am in, but this does not mean that I use weak attacks. If I apply the principles of the rear naked choke whenever I attack, even without the hooks, I can capitalize on the smallest of openings and finish the fight. In this technique, I demonstrate how to do just that. My opponent escapes my back control but leaves his neck exposed, so I transition to a variation of the rear naked choke and finish my opponent right when he is beginning to believe that he is out of danger.

I am controlling Henrique with the seatbelt and with two hooks.

I drag Henrique to my right, aiming to put him on his right side to reduce his mobility and to set up a finish.

As Henrique falls, he cups my right heel with his right hand and begins to remove my right hook.

4

As my right foot slides off of Henrique's right thigh, he lifts his hips and shrimps over my right leg.

5

Recognizing that Henrique has escaped his hips, I release my left hook and plant my left foot on the mat behind me. I would rather abandon my remaining hook and use the seatbelt to reset my back position than allow him to suck me into his half guard.

6

As I begin to reset back control, I see that Henrique has left his neck exposed. I jam my right arm into his neck without hesitation.

7

I lock my hands together, my left palm facing up, and circle my hips away from Henrique.

Without loosening my choke, I swivel behind Henrique, turning my stomach to the mat as I align my body with his.

As I sprawl my legs out to rest my stomach on the mat, I set the back of Henrique's head against my right shoulder to trap him in position for the choke.

Moving one leg at a time, I come up to my knees. As I make that transition, I suck my arms to my chest, driving my forearm into Henrique's neck to finish the fight.

MG FAST FACT

Many fans think that Marcelo favors the RNC (Rear Naked Choke), however he actually places equal importance on the North South. In fact, he says is a higher percentage finish.

MGInAction.com

TAKEDOWNS

Brazilian jiu-jitsu has evolved rapidly in the last decade. As the art grew in popularity around the world, martial artists from a variety of disciplines began to cross-train in jiu-jitsu, like top level judokas and Olympic-level wrestlers. These athletes pushed the sport to a new level by bringing a different kind of talent to the mat, forcing jiu-jitsu fighters—who typically are not known for having exceptional takedowns—to develop an aspect of their game that had been lacking. At the highest levels, giving your opponent two points or even an advantage could mean losing the fight. In addition, fighting from the top is more advantageous than fighting from the bottom in terms of leverage and mechanics. To be a complete grappler, you must learn takedowns.

Every match begins with you and your opponent standing. If you do not have a takedown game, you are putting yourself at an immediate disadvantage that begins the second you touch hands to start the fight. I have said time and time again that my goal is to control the pace through aggression, forcing my opponent to react to my attacks so that all he can do is defend. I never want to allow my opponent to dictate the action of the match.

That same philosophy applies to all aspects of grappling, including the wrestling aspect. To be a well-rounded fighter, I could not just learn to sprawl. To beat a wrestler, I had to learn to wrestle—the single-leg, the double-leg, the clinch. At the same time, I knew that the wrestlers I was competing against had been perfecting their art since they were young and had reached the top of their sport because of their exceptional talent. Expecting to reach their level of experience in a few years was an unreasonable expectation.

SINGLE-LEGS AND DOUBLE-LEGS

Rather than try to master the whole scope of wrestling, which I knew would take a lifetime, I searched for a series of practical techniques that formed a takedown system, allowing me to start with one technique and transition to the next and the next as my opponent defends. To make the most of my takedown system, I needed it to connect with my arm drag system. Since the arm drag frequently leads to the single-leg, I knew that it should be a part of my takedown game. That way, my ability to finish the single-leg would be strong, no matter how I set it up, improving two facets of my game at the same time. If you look ahead to the techniques in this chapter, however, you will notice that my system starts with a double-leg. When you shoot directly for the single-leg, you're limiting your ability to continue attacking. If your opponent sprawls to escape your single, you are stuck beneath your opponent's weight trying to counter his sprawl. I prefer to start by shooting a double-leg because it forces me

to take a stronger shot, putting me deep beneath my opponent's base. If he does defend, transitioning to the single-leg will be easier because he is occupied with fending off the double.

My takedown game is never going to be as elaborate as a career wrestler's, but by perfecting a series of interconnected techniques and connecting them with my arm drag system, I can fight aggressively and with confidence. When I feel that I am unable to outwrestle my opponent, I can fall back on my seated guard game, but my mentality from the seated guard is the same as my mentality from standing. I want to take my opponent down and get on top, as soon as possible, however possible.

THE CLINCH

I chose to incorporate wrestling into my skill set rather than judo because I knew that wrestling techniques were equally applicable to gi and no gi. If I had mastered a series of judo sweeps and throws that relied on gi grips for leverage and feints, I might not have been able to apply those techniques to a no-gi setting. With wrestling, a double-leg is a double-leg regardless of what uniform my opponent is wearing. The clinch, while often an unavoidable aspect of stand-up grappling, is a position that I primarily use in no-gi. In the gi, closing the distance to secure a tie-up is difficult because my opponent can grab anywhere on my gi top to stop my forward motion, so I focus on setting up arm drags and takedowns.

Without the gi, a scramble or a failed shot can quickly result in an over-under clinch, and with no gi grips available, it is not uncommon for both fighters to choose to continue fighting from the clinch. The clinch can be a difficult position to escape, and if your clinch game is weak, you will quickly be on your back in a bad position. As you work through the clinch section, you will notice that my clinch game is like my takedown system: simple and efficient. I do not want to spend too much time on my feet because my techniques are strongest on the ground, so my clinch techniques are designed to either get me the takedown or to force my opponent into abandoning the clinch, allowing me to return to my takedown system or to my seated guard.

OUTSIDE LEG TRIP TO DRIVE THROUGH DOUBLE

The double-leg takedown is the strongest takedown you can get off of a shot in terms of leverage and control. Unlike a single-leg or a high crotch, the double-leg takedown gives you control over both of your opponent's legs, and if you close the distance properly, control over his hips as well. This is ideal for compromising your opponent's base and bringing him to the mat because you are able to dominate the entirety of his lower body in one quick, powerful motion. That is not say that other takedowns are ineffective and that you should not use them. You certainly should. Keep in mind that the double-leg can be used to set up other types of takedowns. Consider it a staging point, the first step in what could be a longer process.

Henrique and I are standing, each of us looking for a takedown.

I grip fight until I can control both of Henrique's wrists with my hands.

I spread Henrique's arms with my hands, clearing a path for a double-leg takedown.

I sink my hips to change levels and drive forward with my left knee as I continue to control Henrique's wrists so that he cannot counter my takedown attempt with an underhook.

I plant my left knee between Henrique's legs, still driving forward through the takedown.

I step forward onto my right foot, riding the momentum of my shot. Notice that I have not yet released Henrique's wrists.

Confident that my shot has penetrated deep enough to produce a reliable takedown, I release Henrique's wrists and cup the backs of his knees with my hands.

Pushing off of my feet, I plow forward, lifting my hips slightly as I suck Henrique's legs toward my hips.

Pressing my head against Henrique's left side, I turn the corner as I drive forward to increase the leverage of my takedown.

As Henrique lands on his back, I rotate my hips to my left, away from my head, aiming to land in side control.

I finish the takedown in side control, tucking my knees under my hips to control the position.

SPEAR DOUBLE

When you work from the standing position, your opponent knows that you want to take him down. He is wary of a tie-up, and he is acutely aware that you could shoot at any moment. If your opponent knows that you have a strong shot, he will hesitate to engage, back pedal when you come forward, and prevent you from controlling his wrists. While his inactivity may be frustrating, you at least know that you have him on the defensive, which gives you an edge. Continue to work for your shot anyway. Since you cannot control his wrists, dive low between his legs to make it more difficult for him to underhook your arms as you come forward. By committing to a strong dive, you give yourself a great deal of momentum, which can be used to finish the spear double.

Henrique and I are both fighting for grips to set up a takedown or a throw.

I repeatedly attempt to control his wrists to set up a takedown or an arm drag, but he is hesitant to engage. I lift my hands toward his shoulders to trick him into raising his arms.

I sink my hips to change levels and begin to drive my left knee forward, intending to shoot my head between Henrique's legs.

I kick off of my right foot to launch myself forward, closing the distance, hooking Henrique's heels with my hands as my head drives between his legs. The force of this movement will slam my shoulders into his shins as I come forward.

I finish my takedown by continuing to drive off of my left foot while swinging my right leg over my head like a scorpion tail. At the same time, I pull backward on Henrique's heels, collapsing his base.

When Henrique hits the mat, I maintain control of his legs, limiting his movement to protect myself from potential counters.

As I crawl my knees under my body, I hop my hands to Henrique's thighs, giving me more control of his legs.

I bring my left knee in and kneel. I can now pass Henrique's guard.

MG FAST FACT

Marcelo prefers to use wrestling style takedowns as opposed to judo style takedowns. Wrestling style takedowns translate better for both gi and no gi.

HELPFUL HINT

The Double Leg Takedown is a favorite of Marcelo's. See all of his variations by using the tree: Standup / Takedowns / Double Leg Takedown

MGInAction.com

SINGLE-LEG TAKEDOWN

The double-leg takedown may be the strongest takedown from a leverage standpoint, but it can also be one of the more difficult takedowns to get. Using a shot to close the distance on an experienced grappler is a challenge in itself. Wrapping both legs once inside, especially if your opponent begins to defend, can sometimes be impossible. If your opponent anticipates the technique, he can step a leg back out of reach with relative ease. A similar situation can occur if your opponent is standing in a southpaw position, with his right foot forward instead of his left. In that case as well, his back leg is too far away for you to establish a double-leg. Whether your opponent is stepping a leg back to prevent the double-leg takedown or he starts in the southpaw position, always shoot with the mind-set of a double-leg takedown, even if a single-leg takedown is your intent. Because the single-leg is a closer target, many grapplers will unknowingly take a weaker shot because they think that they have less distance to travel. Do not make this mistake. When you shoot, aim for the same depth of penetration as a double-leg regardless of what takedown you use in the end.

Henrique and I are on our feet, grip fighting.

I secure both of Henrique's wrists with my hands. I see that he is standing in a southpaw stance, so I know that the double-leg is not an option unless I switch my stance as well.

As I spread Henrique's arms away from his body, I sink my hips and drive my left knee forward to begin my shot.

Shooting as deep as I can, I plant my left knee on the mat next to Henrique's right foot, controlling his wrists throughout the initial shot to prevent him from countering with underhooks.

Releasing Henrique's wrists, I plant my head against the inside of his right thigh and wrap my arms around his right leg.

I drive into Henrique, stepping my right foot forward for additional leverage.

I stand, hugging Henrique's right leg to my chest.

When I reach my feet, I pinch Henrique's right leg between my legs.

To take Henrique down, I step my right foot out to my right and step my left foot back, pointing my toes outward.

As I circle away from Henrique, I pressure down on his leg with my chest and head, forcing him to fall to the mat.

I pull my knees beneath me and rest my weight on Henrique's right leg, ready to pass his guard and win the fight.

SINGLE-LEG TRIP

The single-leg is one of my favorite takedowns, since I can use a variety of moves to set it up—a double-leg, an arm drag, a butterfly sweep, x-guard—but if my opponent is an experienced wrestler, I may have trouble finishing the takedown with the previous technique. He will hop around on his free leg, push my head away, and wiggle his foot free from between my legs. All of these movements create separation between my opponent and me, lessening the strength of my position and thus the chance of my finishing the single-leg. If I wait too long to act, his defense will become offense, and I could find myself being taken down instead. As soon as I feel that the traditional single-leg finish is not going to work, I rotate the other direction and lift my opponent's leg into the air, kicking out his other leg. This is good jiu-jitsu. Do not waste energy fighting your opponent's resistance. Switch to another technique, and if he resists that technique, switch back to the first.

I am attacking Henrique's right leg with a single-leg takedown. His right leg is pinched between my legs, and my head is on the inside of his thigh. I attempted my conventional single-leg takedown, but he is defending by hopping on his foot and pushing me away with his right hand.

I accept that I've lost the traditional single-leg, so I lift my chest and begin to lift Henrique's right leg into the air.

Straightening my back, I hoist Henrique's right leg as high as I can.

I shuffle my right leg toward Henrique, moving my hips closer to his.

I swing my left leg up until my left thigh is flush against his groin and hip. If I attempt to trip Henrique below his knee, he could hop over my leg and remain standing.

6

I kick my left leg back to sweep Henrique's leg. I do so with force, and my kick does not stop until my left leg is behind my right. If I stop halfway through, he could land on my left knee, which could lead to injury.

7

As Henrique falls face-first on the mat, I maintain control of his right leg.

8

I drop Henrique's right leg and shoot forward.

As my right knee slides across the back of Henrique's right leg, I loop my right arm over his right shoulder and my left arm under his left armpit. They meet in the middle to secure the seatbelt. At the same time, I kick my left leg into the air, swinging it over my right.

Henrique turtles, and I settle into position next to him. With my seatbelt locked, I can take his back and set my hooks.

MG FAST FACT

Marcelo likes to use the single leg takedown because it's a very effective technique against larger, stronger opponents. This is because when executed properly, you can load all of your opponent's weight onto a single post (their opposite leg) so that there is only one point of attack to focus on.

HELPFUL HINT

If you enjoyed this technique, watch this variation on MGInAction.com:
Video ID 5431 Or Stand up / Takedowns / Offense / Ankle Pick Takedown / Collar Control from Standing, Ankle Pick Takedown, Pumphandle Gi Grip from Standing, Single Leg Takedown

MGInAction.com

FAILED DOUBLE TO BACKDOOR FINISH (COUNTER SPRAWL)

Even if your shot is quick and your transitions are strong, you must be prepared to cope with the sprawl. None of your takedown techniques will be new to a high-level grappler, and your opponent is thinking of sprawling even before you can change levels to take a shot. If he is faster than you, there is a significant chance that he will sprawl before you can establish the necessary control to finish a double or a single. If you took a good shot, though, you can still get the takedown by going out the backdoor, which will surprise an opponent fixated on defending the single or double. For this technique to work, your shot must carry you far beneath your opponent's base. A shallow shot will leave you unable to counter his sprawl, which is one of the reasons why I have advocated the double-leg mind-set so strongly. When you shoot, you should be thinking of blasting through your opponent. If you do not shoot strong and hard, you can very quickly find yourself in a bad position.

1

Henrique and I are battling for dominant grips.

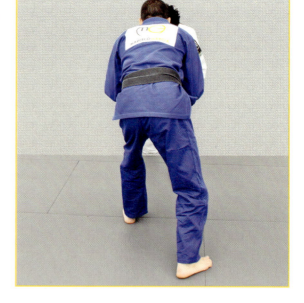

2

I latch on to Henrique's wrists and push his arms away from his body.

I sink my hips to change levels and drive my left knee forward to initiate my shot.

I plant my left knee between Henrique's legs and wrap my arms around his legs to set up a double-leg takedown.

Before I can finish the takedown, Henrique sprawls, kicking his legs behind him as he sinks his hips to the mat.

6

Releasing Henrique's right leg but continuing to control his left, I drive my head between his legs before he can finish his sprawl.

7

I capitalize on my position by pulling my right knee in beneath me and sitting up, lifting Henrique off of the mat. If my shot had been shallow, I would never have been able to reach this point.

8

As I continue to sit up, I grip the back of Henrique's right knee with my left hand for additional control.

I tip my right shoulder to my right while simultaneously pulling down with my right hand and pushing up with my left hand, guiding Henrique's weight over my right shoulder.

I rotate my chest toward the mat as Henrique falls off of my back.

I drop my chest on Henrique's torso to finish the takedown and establish side control.

SINGLE-LEG TO SIT-OUT SWITCH (COUNTER SPRAWL)

SHOOTING IN

In the previous technique, I countered my opponent's sprawl by going out the backdoor, which required me to drape my opponent's weight over my shoulder before bringing him to the mat. While I like using that technique and find it very effective, it can also be difficult to execute against a much larger opponent. Whenever you're attempting to overcome a significant weight disadvantage, you should think more about how you can move around your opponent instead of how you can move your opponent. If I feel that I cannot lift an opponent over my shoulder to go out the back door, I use a sit-out to sneak underneath him, which gives me an avenue to claim the seatbelt, which is actually better for me than landing in side control after a successful takedown. As you will see in the sequence below, this technique is shown from a single-leg position, but it is just as useful if you initially opened with a double-leg.

1 I am on my feet, looking to open the match with a successful takedown.

2 I grab Henrique's wrists with both hands and force them away from his body to clear a path for a single-leg takedown.

I sink my hips and drive my left knee forward to begin my shot.

When my left knee hits the mat, I wrap my arms around Henrique's right leg.

Henrique begins to sprawl, shooting his legs back away from me as he drives his hips to the mat. Before his hips can hit the mat, I force my head as deep between his legs as I can.

6

I step up onto my left foot and post on my right forearm, attempting to fling Henrique over my shoulders like I did in the previous technique, but he is too heavy and balances on his left leg.

7

Without hesitation, I perform a sit-out by sliding my right knee between my right arm and left leg as I pull back on Henrique's right leg with my left hand.

8

Looking up and over my right shoulder, I turn to the right and put my butt on the mat. At the same time, I hug Henrique's right leg and pinch my head against his thigh as I maneuver through the sit-out.

I turn my chest to the back of Henrique's right thigh, swinging my right arm to my right and rowing his right leg toward my hip with my left arm to help me sit up.

When I reach a kneeling position, I release Henrique's right leg and jump forward to establish the seatbelt.

I lock the seatbelt by draping my right arm over Henrique's right shoulder, shooting my left arm under his left armpit, and grabbing my right wrist with my left hand. I finish the transition by posting my feet to his right side, giving me multiple options for taking his back.

SECURING THE OVER-UNDER CLINCH

Typically, I will avoid fighting from the clinch because the clinch game tends to favor a larger and stronger opponent. If I feel that my opponent and I are equal in terms of size and strength, then there is a chance that I will initiate the clinch to slow him down. Remember, I only use the clinch in no-gi. Transitioning to an over-under position in the gi is difficult because my opponent can use a variety of grips to stop me. Should you like fighting from the over-under clinch, you could certainly use the techniques in this section with the gi, but I recommend devoting training to grip fighting instead.

Henrique and I are squared off and fighting for the takedown.

I grab Henrique's wrists, but I feel that he is too fast for me to shoot. I decide that I need to use the over-under clinch to slow him down.

Without releasing Henrique's wrists, I step forward, pressing my right shoulder against his right shoulder.

I swim my right arm into an underhook and overhook Henrique's right arm with my left arm, gripping his triceps.

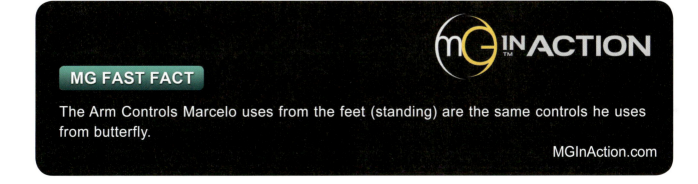

MG IN ACTION

MG FAST FACT

The Arm Controls Marcelo uses from the feet (standing) are the same controls he uses from butterfly.

MGInAction.com

SINGLE-LEG SCOOP

The challenge of working from the over-under clinch is that neither you nor your opponent have a superior position. He has the exact same position as you, so the match could quickly degenerate to a battle of strength, which could be bad for you if you happen to be smaller. The key to not getting bullied in the clinch is to have a plan, a series of techniques that you can immediately throw at your opponent to put him on the defensive, and I recommend starting with the single-leg scoop. The single-leg scoop is the first technique that I attempt from the over-under clinch because it is simple, quick, and effective. If it fails, I am in position to counter my opponent's resistance with other techniques. Like all techniques in this book, the single-leg scoop works best when used as part of a system. If your opponent blocks it, transition to the next technique in the series right away.

Henrique and I start in the over-under clinch. I am underhooking his left armpit with my right arm, and I am overhooking his left arm, clamping on to his right elbow with my left hand.

I dip my left shoulder to the side and lift my right shoulder, using my body weight and the strength of my right underhook to twist Henrique's torso. At the same time, I reach my left hand behind his right leg and cup the back of his right knee.

I step forward with my left leg and drive off of my right foot, propelling myself into Henrique as I scoop his left leg between mine with my left hand. In this step, I use the momentum of my drive to lift his leg, not my arm strength.

I continue moving forward, forcing Henrique to fall because he can no longer use his right leg as a support.

I land in Henrique's half guard with my head to the right side of his head.

I plant my left knee on the mat to establish my base. I am now in a great position to use a classic cross knee pass to blow through Henrique's half guard.

OVER-UNDER CLINCH

FAILED SINGLE-LEG SCOOP TO DROP SWEEP

The single-leg scoop is like a jab. I throw it with confidence and with every intention of landing it, but I anticipate my opponent defending. Even though it may not land, let alone end the fight, the single-leg scoop forces my opponent to react. As I have said before in this book, my opponent has a finite amount of techniques he can use to defend a particular attack, and by predicting his next move, I can transition to my next counter while he is still defending my first. When I attempt the single-leg scoop, I know that the majority of grapplers will respond with a simple, instinctual reaction: stepping their leg back away from my reaching arm. By stepping away to stop the single-leg scoop, my opponent stretches himself out, creating a substantial amount of space between us. I then use the over-under clinch to drag my opponent to the mat and use a butterfly hook to sweep him onto his back. Once you master the mechanics of this sequence, proper timing will become the true key to success. You should use the drop sweep the instant that your opponent steps away from the single-leg scoop, catching him in between stances where he is the most vulnerable.

Henrique and I are in the over-under clinch position. I lift with my right underhook and dip my left shoulder to twist Henrique's torso, cupping the back of his right knee with my left hand to initiate the single-leg scoop.

Henrique senses that he is in danger of being taken down and kicks his right leg back, breaking free of my left-hand grip.

3

I latch on to Henrique's right elbow with my left hand and pinch my left elbow into my ribs to trap his arm without allowing him to straighten his back.

4

I step my left foot forward into the space where Henrique's right foot used to be.

5

I drop my hips to the mat, leaning to my left as I straighten my left leg.

6

As my left side hits the mat, I hook the inside of Henrique's left leg with my right foot, establishing a butterfly hook. Notice how I am turned to my left. If I fall flat on my back, I will not have enough leverage to sweep.

7

Turning my chest to the mat, I kick my right foot over my left shoulder, elevating Henrique's hips and turning his back toward the mat. Maintaining the over-under clinch position throughout the sweep is essential. If I do not, Henrique could post his right arm to block my sweep in this step.

8

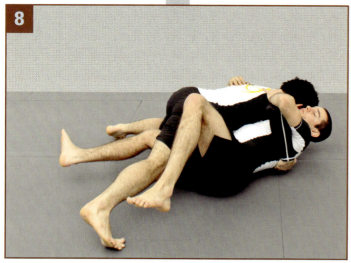

I follow Henrique as his back falls to the mat and use the over-under clinch position to pin him into place.

COUNTERING DOUBLE UNDERHOOKS

Giving your opponent double underhooks in the clinch position can be a disastrous mistake. With double underhooks, your opponent has full control of your upper body and access to your lower body. When fighting from the over-under clinch, you should do your best to prevent your opponent from pummeling his overhook arm into an underhook, but at the same time, having a plan for when things go wrong is just as important as having a plan for when things go right. To salvage a takedown when your opponent secures a second underhook, you must counter before his underhook is completely set. If his second underhook is sunk deep, you have very few reliable counters at your disposal.

Henrique and I are in the over-under clinch position.

Henrique slides his left hand toward his chest to begin pummeling his left arm into an underhook.

3

To slip his left arm between our chests, Henrique creates separation and points his left hand downward, looping it over the outside of my right arm and to the inside. Note how he is forced to lean to his right to pummel his left arm in. I intend to use that lean against him later in the technique.

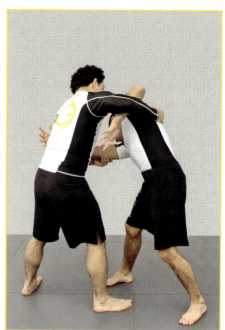

4

Before Henrique can completely set his left underhook, I lock my hands together, squeezing my arms together to stop his left elbow from sliding around to my back and to prevent him from regaining posture.

5

Continuing to squeeze my arms together, I step my right foot between Henrique's legs, pointing my toes toward his right instep, and I step my left foot next to my right, pointing my toes away from him. This footwork turns my chest away from him.

While balancing on my left foot, I lift my right leg and swing it above Henrique's right knee.

I simultaneously twist to my left and kick my right leg back as hard as I can, sweeping Henrique's legs.

I follow Henrique to the mat and land in side control.

To settle my position, I pummel my right arm under his left arm, shoot my left arm behind his head, and lock my hands together. At the same time, I tuck my knees against his right side and lower my hips.

ATTACKING THE GUARD

I always want to be in the top position. Always. My entire game is built around sweeping my opponent and getting on top where I can use agility, positioning, and gravity to overwhelm my opponent's defenses. In the previous chapters, I demonstrated how to use arm drags and takedowns to put your opponent on his back, and in my previous book, *The X-Guard*, I detailed my entire system for sweeping my opponent with the butterfly guard and the x-guard. Those are all methods for getting to the top, but the key to a successful top game is guard passing. A successful takedown will often land you in your oppo-

nent's guard, and your opponent will never stop trying to reclaim his guard when he is on the bottom. If you cannot pass the guard, your top game is worthless.

As you saw in the arm drag chapter, a relatively simple technique quickly branches into a series of counters and re-counters. By familiarizing yourself with the most common counters to your techniques, you can have your re-counter prepared, allowing you to attack with a new technique while your opponent is still defending your first. This is how you force your opponent to play your game, and this is also how you get ahead of your opponent. The same philosophy applies to the way I pass guard. I pass with speed and with aggression, flowing from one technique to the next, but that does not mean that I am reckless. If my technique is sloppy, I will fall into a submission. To be both fast and technical, you have to drill a guard pass over and over, increasing the speed of your pass as you refine and perfect the details of the move.

The guard, however, is a complex position. One guard pass is unlikely to be enough to get you through the guard and to side control. Instead, approach passing the guard in stages.

BREAKING THE CLOSED GUARD

Being trapped in the closed guard can be dangerous, and it wastes precious match time. Competitive grapplers tend to be athletic, so they can hold the closed guard indefinitely, which can mean defeat if you are behind on points. To open the guard and begin to pass, I prefer to stand to maximize the leverage of my techniques. The pressure is simply too great for my opponent to resist. The challenge of opening the closed guard by standing is that your opponent will immediately attack your legs, attempting to counter your guard break with a sweep. I have included techniques to troubleshoot this problem, but you will still need to practice these techniques against a resisting opponent to develop your balance. I can assure you, however, that these guard breaks are effective, as I have successfully used them time and time again against world-class competitors.

PASSING THE OPEN GUARD

Your opponent's approach to closed guard will typically be relatively straightforward. The nature of closed guard limits his options for attacking, but open guard is a different beast entirely. Approaches to open guard vary dramatically from grappler to grappler, and you can easily be overwhelmed by the variations in grips and leg positioning. Instead of waiting for my opponent to start playing his game, I immediately impose mine. To limit my opponent's attack options, I control his hip with one hand and press one of his knees to the mat with the other hand, angling his

I still want to pass with speed, but I need to adjust my approach to account for the change in position. The hand placement that I used to control my opponent's hips to pass his open guard puts me in position to dominate his legs and pass his half guard. If for some reason I am forced to my knees, my strategy for passing the half guard is in keeping with traditional techniques—so keep working to perfect the kneeling half guard passes that you have been using—but I see a lot of grapplers struggle to overcome their opponent securing the underhook from the bottom. Rather than cover a bunch of techniques that you already know, I included my method for countering the underhook from the bottom and turning it into an advantageous position for you. My goal is not to reteach basic techniques but rather to help you see jiu-jitsu the way that I do, so that you can expand and develop your game.

hips to one side or the other. By forcing his hips to face in one direction, I reduce his mobility and force him to defend. If his hips are free, he can play any guard that he wants, so I control his hips as soon as possible and then use my speed to blow through his open guard using the techniques that I demonstrate in this chapter.

PASSING THE HALF GUARD

As much as I would like to open the closed guard, dominate my opponent's hips, and pass the open guard directly to side control, a good competitor will always do his best to prevent me from accomplishing my goal. I may pass the open guard, but I may still get trapped in

UNDERHOOK BREAK

Opening the closed guard is a unique challenge. In most positions, you can threaten submissions to force your opponent to defend, creating openings for you to improve your position. Inside of the guard, however, you have no high-percentage submission options. Any submission options that you do have are more likely to put you in danger than they are to finish the fight. Because of this, many grapplers believe that having the guard is a superior position to being in the guard, but I disagree. If you are trying to pass, you have one advantage that trumps your opponent's submission options: gravity. I prefer to open the closed guard by standing so that I can maximize my use of gravity to create an unstoppable amount of pressure on my opponent's legs. If I attempt a similar guard break from a kneeling position, a larger, stronger opponent can resist what little leverage I can muster. At my school, I instruct my students to use standing guard breaks so that they never have to worry about the strength of their opponent's legs.

I am in Henrique's closed guard. I need to open his legs before I can pass.

I do not waste time hunting for grips. I press my hands against Henrique's chest and lift my hips to jump to my feet.

I stand, bending my knees slightly to center my weight straight up and down rather than leaning forward or backward.

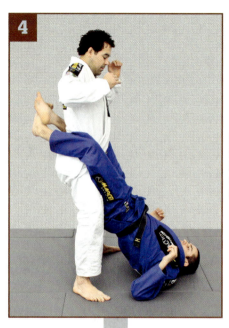

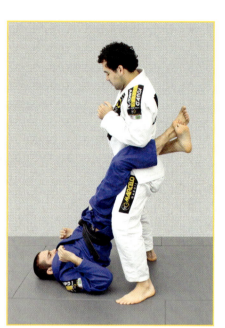

I stand up straight, removing my hands from Henrique's chest and driving my hips slightly forward. As I do that, I lift my arms to prevent him from establishing a grip on my sleeves or upper body.

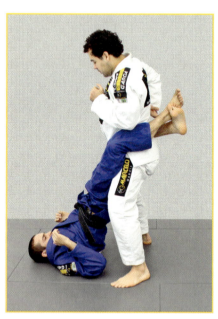

While keeping my left arm out of Henrique's reach, I swim my right arm behind my back.

I shoot my right hand down my back and between Henrique's legs, hooking his left ankle by turning my right palm upward as though I were doing a biceps curl.

7

I jerk my right arm upward to uncross Henrique's ankles.

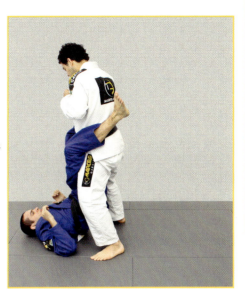

8

As soon as Henrique's guard opens, I step my left leg back to create distance, preventing him from putting me back in guard, and lower my chest, smashing his right knee to the mat with my left hand and cupping his left hip with my right hand. As I control his left hip with my right hand, it is important that I keep my right elbow tucked inside of his left thigh to limit the mobility of his guard.

ALTERNATE HAND POSITIONING

If my right hand is positioned more on Henrique's stomach and ribs instead of hip, that is perfectly okay. I just make sure that my fingers are pointing out. If they are pointing toward his chin, he can wristlock me just by sitting up.

If I am competing in the gi, I could also grab my opponent's lapel with my right hand, but doing so is not always a necessity.

UNDERHOOK BREAK TO SWEEP COUNTER

The underhook break is a powerful, reliable way for breaking the closed guard. Your opponent, however, will rarely give up the position so easily. Standing in the guard puts your upper body out of reach, which makes it easier for you to focus on opening his legs, but your legs are vulnerable. If you stand and your opponent strains to maintain his closed guard, expect him to grab your heels and bridge his hips to attempt to sweep you. Many grapplers abandon standing guard breaks because of this very sweep. An opponent grabbing your heels can be frustrating if you do not know how to properly defend and escape. The key is to ignore the instinct to yank your foot back to free your heel, as making that movement actually makes the sweep easier for your opponent. Instead, kick your foot forward and then circle it away from your opponent's hand. It may seem counterintuitive, but kicking forward moves your foot away from your opponent's hand, rather than into it.

I start in Henrique's closed guard, controlling his chest with my hands.

I lean my weight slightly forward and come up on to my toes.

In one motion, I jump to my feet.

As I straighten my back and pull my arms away from Henrique, he cups my heels to set up a very common sweep from guard.

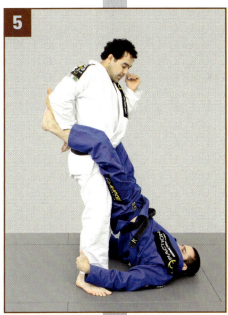

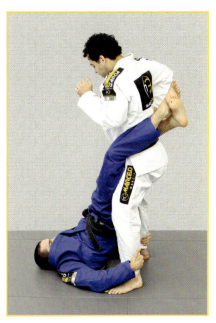

I swim my right arm behind my back and between his legs. I maintain a slight bend in my knees to keep my balance.

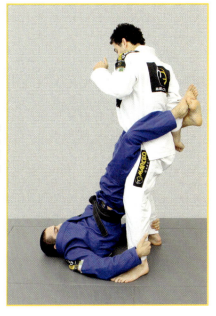

I lean to my right and perform a biceps curl with my right arm to hook Henrique's left ankle. It is important that I lean toward my hooking arm so that I can effectively escape his grips.

7

As I open Henrique's legs with my right arm, I kick my left foot forward and circle it out to my left, escaping his grip.

8

I swing my left foot behind me. As my left leg moves into position, I press Henrique's right knee to the mat with my left hand and control his left hip with my right hand.

---

mG ʰᵐ IN ACTION

MG FAST FACT

Want to see the Video Instructional on MGInAction.com?

Video ID #4768

You can also search in the 'Keyword Search' bar for 'Breaking the Closed Guard' for a variety of related results.

MGInAction.com

ARM PIN UNDERHOOK BREAK

Defending the hip sweep when you stand to open the closed guard is challenging and requires both confidence and practice. If my opponent is larger than me, I anticipate his hip sweep being even stronger than usual, so I take extra precautions to prevent myself from being swept. When I fought Xande Ribeiro in the 2005 ADCC, for example, I knew that the combination of his strength and talent would make me susceptible to sweeps when I stood in the guard. Rather than jump right to a standing guard break, I controlled his biceps and stepped on his arm to pin his shoulders in place while I pried his guard open. Had I given Ribeiro the space to move, he may have swept me, and I might not have won the match, but since my foot was planted on his biceps, he could not counter my guard break. If this technique worked against a grappler of Ribeiro's caliber, then it will work for you too.

I am in Henrique's guard and am controlling his chest with my hands.

To limit Henrique's gripping options, I cup his biceps and pin them in place with my hands. To make this control position effective, I point my elbows in rather than flaring them out.

I lean my weight onto Henrique's arms.

I lift my knees off of the mat, posting on my toes. I do not stand just yet, and I use my body weight to hold Henrique's arms in place.

To stand, I step my left foot forward onto Henrique's right biceps, replacing my left hand. For optimal stability, I favor having my left heel pointing toward the mat, inside of his left arm. If I lift my heel too much, he could escape his arm and attack my leg.

MG IN ACTION

6 I straighten my back and lift my arms to transition to the underhook break, using my left foot to keep Henrique's right arm pinned.

7 I shoot my right arm behind my back and between Henrique's legs.

8 To open his legs, I hook Henrique's left ankle with the crook of my right arm and twist my core.

In one motion, I swing my left leg behind me, cup his left hip with my right hand, and control his right knee with my left hand.

I pin Henrique's right knee to the mat with my left hand to complete the guard break and to set up a guard pass.

KNEE PUSH BREAK

In the previous three techniques, my opponent stayed on his back when I stood to open his guard, and I even pinned his arm to the mat with my foot to prevent him from attacking my legs as I pried his legs apart. Grapplers are exceptional athletes, however, so many of them will sit up with you as you stand, keeping their guard locked as they wrap their arms around you. Most seasoned competitors have the strength and endurance to hold this seemingly awkward position indefinitely. For the person standing, supporting the weight of an opponent is taxing on the legs, especially if that opponent is moving and attacking. When you stand in the guard, do not linger. Do not waste your energy and give your opponent time to attack. Immediately open the guard and work to pass, even if your opponent sits up with you.

I am in Henrique's closed guard, working to open his legs.

Before I can make my move, Henrique grabs my shoulders with both hands, attempting to collapse my posture.

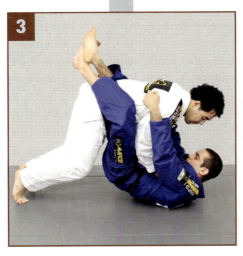

I ignore Henrique's grips and begin to stand by coming up on to my toes, lifting my knees off of the mat.

I come up to my feet, and Henrique clings to my gi.

As I straighten my back to stand, Henrique flexes his abdominals to lift his shoulders off of the mat, sitting up with me.

Henrique wraps his arms around my back to eliminate space and to maintain his guard. To create separation, I slide my hands to the outsides of his hips, and press him away.

Once I have created some space between us, I loop my left arm under Henrique's right armpit and cup his right shoulder with my left hand.

8

Leaning to my left, I maneuver my right hand to the inside of Henrique's left knee.

9

I bounce my hips and push down on Henrique's left knee with my right hand to open his guard.

10

When Henrique's legs open, I step my right foot back and continue to press his left knee to the mat with my right hand. If I relax my pressure before I have pinned his left leg, he could counter.

11

I use my body weight to pin Henrique's left knee to the mat. I am now in a great position to pass.

FOOT-OVER-FOOT PASS

Passing the open guard can be a complex process. The space between you and your opponent is ever changing. Your opponent can transition between multiple guard variations with ease. And if you make a grave mistake, you will be swept or submitted. Do not let your opponent dictate the action. Impose your game on him. Your attitude should be confident and aggressive, and you should pass with speed. The fastest passes tend to be the simplest, so do not transition to a more elaborate guard pass unless you are forced to. One of my favorite passes is the foot-over-foot pass, and even though it is a fundamental guard pass that most white belts learn within their first month, I want to touch on the details that make the pass strong and efficient. I have been using this pass for a long time, and even though it is basic, I love to use it first because I can predict how my opponent will react, which funnels him into playing my game.

I start in Henrique's open guard. I am posting my right hand on his left knee and controlling his right hip with my left hand.

I drive my right knee across Henrique's left thigh while maintaining my hand positioning. I do not slide my right knee to the mat, however. By keeping my right knee off of the mat, I can use all of my body weight to pin his leg.

3

I shoot my left arm under Henrique's right arm, securing an underhook.

4

I lift my left foot and curl it toward my butt.

5

I cross my left foot over my right to prevent Henrique from trapping my left leg in half guard as I pass. It's also important to note that my right shin is still on his left thigh, allowing me to pin his left leg in place as I set my left foot.

6

While keeping my legs crossed, I lift my right foot and swivel my hips to my right to pass my legs over Henrique's left leg, moving my legs as one unit to escape them both simultaneously.

7

I uncross my feet and drive my left knee into Henrique's left hip and drive my right knee into his left shoulder. I wrap my right arm around his head and grip my right hand with my left to establish head and arm control.

KNEE INSIDE PASS

The foot-over-foot pass is a fundamental technique because it is simple, direct, efficient, and effective. Your opponent will likely defend it though—not because the technique is inherently flawed in any way, but because even a white belt knows that when his guard is open you want to pass. As soon as you close the distance, regardless of what move you attempt, your opponent will instinctively shrimp to create space and regain his guard. The beauty of the foot-over-foot pass is that even though your opponent can hip-escape, you are one movement away from the knee inside pass. If you move with speed, your opponent will not realize that you have transitioned to a different technique until you have passed his guard. When you are drilling, couple the two passes, and the quality of your guard pass game will improve.

I am in Henrique's open guard, controlling his left leg and his right hip.

I drive my right knee forward and over Henrique's left thigh, initiating the foot-over-foot pass.

3

Before I can complete the foot-over-foot pass, Henrique posts both hands on my right thigh. I know that his next move is to shrimp away and that I no longer have the correct position to cross my feet and pass.

4

I counter Henrique's escape attempt by sliding my left knee next to my right knee and over his left thigh, beginning the knee inside pass.

5

I lean my hips to my left as I shoot my left knee between Henrique's legs and to the mat on his left side.

6

While resting the majority of my weight on Henrique, I snake my right hand under Henrique's right wrist.

7

I rip Henrique's right hand off of my right thigh by hooking his right arm with my right arm and looping it toward his head.

8

As I force Henrique's right arm toward his head, I hook his head with my right arm and baseball slide off of his left thigh.

9

I sink my chest into Henrique's chest, tucking my knees against my body and using my underhook to stabilize the top position.

MG FAST FACT

The 'Knee Inside Pass' is an effective way to pass the guard in both the gi and no gi. Watch Marcelo demonstrate it here:

Video ID 4378

Guard / Passes / Knee Inside Pass vs. Closed Guard / Breaking the Closed Guard, Knee Slide Pass, Knee Inside Pass vs. Closed Guard

MGInAction.com

X-PASS

The x-pass can come into play if you are unable to pin your opponent's leg to the mat to set up a foot-over-foot pass or a cross-knee pass. If you are transitioning from a standing guard break to one of those passes, pinning his leg should rarely be a problem because you are coming down on his leg from a significant height, using gravity and your body weight simultaneously. I have found that I use the x-pass most often when I am attacking a seated opponent. Because I have to first flatten his back to the mat and then work to pin his legs, I am more likely to fail when I attempt to control his leg like I did in previous passes. I still attempt the foot-over-foot pass first, but I am more than happy to use it as a distraction to set up the x-pass. You will notice that I transition to knee on belly rather than to side control when I attack with the x-pass. Since the majority of the pass is executed from a standing position, rather than a kneeling position, I have to cover a lot of distance with my hips to get them on the mat to secure side control. By transitioning to knee-on-belly first, I can surf my opponent's attempts to escape and then drop into side control in a controlled, methodical manner.

Henrique is in the seated guard position, and I am looking to pass.

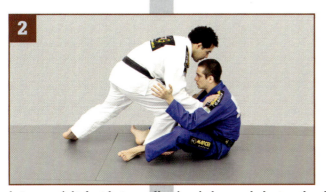

I step my right foot between Henrique's legs and plant my hands against his shoulders.

Stepping forward with my left leg, I shove Henrique onto his back.

I latch on to Henrique's lapel with my right hand to pin him on his back.

I cup Henrique's right knee with my left hand and attempt to pin his right leg to the mat, but he resists.

As soon as I feel that Henrique is fighting me, I shove his right leg between my legs as I kick my right leg behind me.

I kick my leg toward the ceiling like a scorpion tail, and I press Henrique's right leg until it is almost fully extended, exposing his ribs.

Lowering my right leg, I point my knee toward his ribs.

I slide my right knee across Henrique's stomach and post out on my left foot to establish knee-on-belly.

Henrique instantly shrimps away to escape the pressure of my knee.

I use Henrique's escape attempt to drop into side control, shooting my right arm under his left arm and hooking his head with my left arm. I lock my hands together and sink my hips to settle into position.

CROSS-KNEE VARIATION

To counter your x-pass, many opponents will cross their ankles to trap you in a standing half guard position. If that happens to you, do not allow your opponent to slow you down. Continue to pass aggressively and with speed by transitioning to another pass right away. In jiu-jitsu, if your opponent defends one direction of movement, switch to the opposite direction of movement to catch him where he is weak. In this application of the cross-knee pass, you attempt to kick your leg back for the x-pass, and you slam forward the instant that you encounter resistance. Your movement should be fast and explosive to surprise your opponent and beat his guard. If you master switching between the x-pass and the cross-knee pass, your confidence in your guard passing will soar.

I am standing in Henrique's half guard, gripping his lapel with my right hand and controlling his right knee with my left hand. His ankles are crossed.

I attempt the x-pass by kicking my right leg back. Though Henrique blocks me, moving my leg backward stretches him out and creates space, which I can use to execute the cross-knee pass.

I shove Henrique's right knee between my legs with my left hand as I point my right knee and shoot it forward over his right hip.

I continue to slide my right knee through Henrique's legs, popping my hips forward to create momentum.

Leading with my hips and legs, I slide through Henrique's guard. Notice that my hips are moving toward the mat to his right. If my hips are too much on his body, he could roll me to his left.

Continuing to slide forward, I snake my right arm under Henrique's left arm to establish an underhook.

I complete the pass by turning my chest to his, locking my hands together, and tucking my knees against his ribs.

FORCING THE CROSS-KNEE PASS

Even though the cross-knee pass is an explosive movement, a strong opponent can resist the forward momentum of your knee and hips by pinching his knees together. If his ankles are still crossed, transitioning back into the x-pass is pointless. Before you decide to switch to the next pass variation that I show after the cross-knee series, which is the smash pass, attempt to force your way through your opponent's legs by using both hands to shuck his knees. In many situations, that will give you enough additional leverage to complete the cross-knee pass. Even though adjusting your grips to shuck both of his legs at once will create a slight pause in your technique, the cross-knee pass itself should still be explosive and powerful. Attempting to force your knee through slowly will leave you vulnerable to counters and sweeps.

I am standing with my right leg trapped in Henrique's half guard. I am controlling his lapel with my right hand and his right knee with my left hand.

I set up the cross-knee pass by first attempting the x-pass, kicking my right leg backward to create space.

3

Transitioning to the cross-knee pass, I attempt to shoot my right knee between Henrique's legs, but he clamps his knees together in front of my knee to block me.

4

Before abandoning the cross-knee pass, I decide to try forcing my way through by cupping the tops of Henrique's knees with both hands.

5

In one motion, I shuck Henrique's knees away from his body with my hands and pop my knee forward, removing the obstacle that was blocking my pass.

Without releasing Henrique's knees, I thrust my hips, angling my right knee across his right hip as I move through his guard.

I baseball slide out of Henrique's legs, dragging my right hip across the mat.

I loop my right arm under Henrique's left arm, and I wrap my left arm around his head.

I turn my chest toward the mat, lock my hands, and sink my hips to complete the pass and establish side control.

HELPFUL HINT

Marcelo often uses his passes in combination. The tagging system on MGInAction will help lead you to any related techniques that naturally precede or follow a failed or successful primary attempt. Try searching for your favorite pass on MGInAction.com and before you click on a video, look at the bottom of the description on the search results page to see what other techniques fit in well with your query.

MGInAction.com

COUNTER SINGLE-LEG CONTROL WITH STEP-OVER PASS

If your opponent pinches his legs together to block the cross-knee pass, you can expect him to cling to your leg with what resembles a deep half guard or a single-leg position as you drive through his guard. In terms of your vulnerability in this position, you are relatively safe as long as you do not allow him to transition to his knees. Even if you are able to keep your opponent on his side, his death grip can be frustrating if you do not have a strategy for escaping it. My preferred countermeasure is to execute a step-over pass, switching my hips to the opposite side. From that position, my opponent can no longer turn to his knees, and I can use my other leg to peel him off of me. You will see me use a variation of this technique in the kneeling half guard section because it is one of my favorite methods to pass, and I use it all the time.

I am standing in Henrique's half guard, gripping his lapel and controlling his knee.

I shuck Henrique's right knee and begin to slide my right knee between his legs to initiate the cross-knee pass.

As I cross Henrique's right hip with my right knee, he turns on to his side and wraps his arms around my right leg.

Realizing that my cross-knee pass will not be clean and simple, I post both hands on the mat.

I switch my hips to the opposite side of Henrique's body by lifting my left leg and kicking it behind me.

MG IN ACTION

6

As I swing my left leg behind me, I allow my hips to turn to face Henrique's leg and sink my butt to the mat.

7

I land on my butt with my left leg curled under me to strengthen my base.

8

To weaken Henrique's position, I point my fingers and snake my right hand under his right armpit.

I lean forward to force my right arm under his right arm.

Continuing the motion of the previous step, I drive my right arm backward into Henrique's right arm to break his grip on my leg and to flare his right elbow away from his ribs.

With my right forearm parallel to the mat, I grab as high as I can on Henrique's upper back to trap his right arm against his face. In this position, his right arm is almost completely useless.

I grab Henrique's right pant leg with my left hand and post my left foot on the mat to shrimp my hips away, sliding as much of my right leg out from between his legs as I can.

With only my right ankle trapped between Henrique's legs, I set my left foot on his left knee.

Extending my left leg, I pry Henrique's half guard off of my right ankle.

15

Dropping my right leg on the mat, I scissor my left leg behind me.

16

I swivel my right leg under my left, circling my hips toward Henrique's head.

17

I transition to north-south by dropping my chest on Henrique's chest and hugging his upper torso with my elbows.

SMASH PASS

Passing the open guard is hectic, and becoming entangled in your opponent's legs is easy. Consequently, you can find yourself standing in your opponent's half guard for a variety of reasons, especially if you used the series that I taught previously in this chapter. By wrapping and hooking one of your legs, your opponent can protect himself from the foot-over-foot pass, the x-pass, and the cross-knee pass. In the standing half guard, you still have the superior position, but if you do not attack, your opponent will, and you should never let your opponent force you to defend. When your x-pass and cross-knee pass fail, immediately grip the outside of your opponent's knee and shove it into his other knee, forcing his hips to rotate toward your trapped leg. The driving principle behind my standing pass game is to constantly attack my opponent's legs from different angles. It is impossible for him to defend all angles at once, so I constantly switch the direction of my pressure until I catch him.

I am standing in Henrique's open guard. I am pinning him on his back by gripping his lapel with my right hand and am looking to pass.

I cup the top of Henrique's right knee with my left hand to attempt the x-pass, but he crosses his ankles to defend. I do not feel that I have the space to execute the cross-knee pass, so I opt to transition to the smash pass.

3

I switch my left hand to the outside of Henrique's right knee.

4

As I smash Henrique's right knee across his body and into his left knee, I shift my hips laterally, pointing my right knee out as I sink to my right.

5

I drop my chest on Henrique's right thigh to lock his legs in place and swim my left arm around his back to set up an underhook later in the sequence. My right knee is still between his legs, trapped between his right shin and left calf, but he is in a weak position and has very little control or leverage that he can use against me.

6

I sprawl my right leg back to further extend Henrique's legs, making them even weaker.

7

I curl my left foot to my butt and hook Henrique's right foot. I do not necessarily need to lace my toes in front of his ankle. I just need to establish enough contact to be able to manipulate his right leg.

8

I press my left foot to the mat to pin Henrique's right foot as I lift my hips and kick my right leg free.

While still pinning Henrique's right foot, I lift my hips and hop to my left, toward his back.

I land behind Henrique, but am still somewhat low on his body.

To climb higher on Henrique, I post on the balls of my feet and shoot my chest up his chest.

I bring my left knee into Henrique's right armpit to complete my pass and achieve a strong side control position.

MG FAST FACT

Marcelo believes in mastering certain techniques on certain sides. For example, he tends to use standing passes to his left, and a low over-under when he goes to the right. He does this because if every technique were practiced equally on both sides, he might only realize 50% of his ability to each side. By selecting a natural side for each technique and choosing to dedicate 100% of his drilling time to it, he can optimally focus on developing his muscle memory, thus improving his understanding and application.

MGInAction.com

SMASH TO HALF GUARD TO CROSS-KNEE PASS VARIATION

For any of the previous techniques to be effective, my opponent must be willing to engage. If my opponent scoots away every time I step toward his seated guard, I risk overextending myself and walking into a trap. To attack an evasive opponent, I need to cover a great deal of distance very quickly. To accomplish that, I perform a movement that closely resembles a shot, but rather than latching on to his legs, I sink an underhook and dive through his half guard, finishing with a classic variation of the cross-knee pass to beat his half guard. Do not be intimidated by the complexity of this technique. At its core, it is composed of simple movements that you have seen used throughout this book, and as you practice it, you may be surprised at how quickly it comes to you. When you go for it in a match, commit to it completely. Hesitation will weaken your technique.

I am standing, working to pass Henrique's seated guard. Each time I come forward, he scoots away.

I sink my hips to change levels.

I shoot in, driving my right knee forward as I aim to snake my right arm under his left.

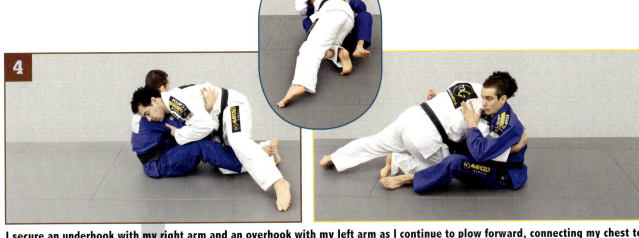

I secure an underhook with my right arm and an overhook with my left arm as I continue to plow forward, connecting my chest to Henrique's chest. Notice how my head is to the right of his head. My head positioning is an essential part of the pass.

As I drive Henrique's back to the mat, I step my left leg out wide to avoid his full guard.

I flatten Henrique out, sinking my hips and sprawling my legs. If a portion of my hips are on his body, I scoot them off to the side so that my stomach is as flat to the mat as possible. By posting my head to the right of his head, I greatly weaken the strength of his underhook.

Without lifting my hips, I pull my left leg in, sliding it across the mat as my left knee bends. I then post my left foot on top of Henrique's right knee.

As I kick Henrique's right leg away with my foot, I raise my hips and begin pulling my right leg free.

I completely escape my right leg by executing a cross-knee pass, baseball sliding my hips away from Henrique.

I pull on Henrique's right triceps and push off of the mat with my left foot to prevent him from turning into me as I transition to side control.

I face my chest and hips toward the mat to secure side control.

COUNTER UNDERHOOK TO SHIN BLOCK HALF GUARD PASS

When I pass the half guard from the kneeling position, I incorporate the same principles that I use to pass the half guard when I am standing. I am just working with less space. If I have the underhook, I will use the latter portion of the previous technique to escape my trapped leg. If I do not have the underhook, I need to nullify his leverage advantage as quickly as possible or my opponent could counter my pass. To shut down his underhook, I use a position similar to the step-over pass to weaken and trap his arm. This concept, threading your opposite arm under your opponent's underhook, is an integral part of my system. I have made it second nature, and I use it constantly. As you experiment with the position, remember to counter your opponent's underhook as early as possible. You will have much more success battling a shallow underhook than a deep one, so work to stay ahead of your opponent by anticipating his intentions.

I am kneeling in Henrique's half guard, working to free my left leg. I attempt to set my left underhook, but I see that he is going to set his right underhook before I can.

Henrique swims his right arm under my left armpit. To prevent him from shooting his elbow all the way through, I clamp my left arm against his body to trap his right forearm under my left arm.

Without releasing the pressure I am applying with my left arm, I snake my right hand under his right armpit.

I jam my right arm forward as I swivel my right hip toward the mat. With my right arm wedged under Henrique's right arm, his underhook is no longer effective.

As my right hip hits the mat, I drive my right elbow back to flare Henrique's right arm away from his body.

MG IN ACTION

Facing Henrique's legs, I grip his thigh with my left hand and shrimp my hips away from his, creating space and forcing my right arm even higher on his body. Once I am confident that his right arm is no longer a threat, I grab a clump of gi fabric on his upper back to secure the position.

I slide my right knee into the space that I created in the previous step and set my right shin against the top of Henrique's left thigh.

I press Henrique's right thigh away with my left hand as I shrimp again, scooting my hips up his side to begin freeing my left leg.

9

When only my left foot is trapped between Henrique's legs, I straighten and scissor my legs to stretch him out even more.

10

I point my toes and slip my left foot free.

11

I swing my left leg behind me and post it on the mat to keep from rolling to my back.

Since I do not have control of Henrique's head, I begin to transition to north-south by sliding my right leg under my left, rotating my hips toward his head as I turn my chest to his.

I pull my knees under my hips and sink my weight to stabilize the top position, ready to attack with a north-south guillotine.

FLATTEN OPPONENT TO TORNADO PASS

The butterfly guard is unlike the closed guard or half guard. In the butterfly guard, your opponent is not trying to hold you in place. It is a dynamic open guard position that is mostly used to set up sweeps. If I am struggling to pass my opponent's guard, I will sometimes enter his butterfly guard voluntarily because I am confident in my base and my ability to pass from the position. Since I know how to nullify the leverage of the butterfly hooks, I can enter the position, protect myself from sweeps, and quickly pass with the tornado pass. Admittedly, the tornado pass is a high-level technique, and it requires an advanced level of coordination and finesse to execute properly. It looks flashy, but if you have seen me grapple, you know that I only use the most effective techniques. The tornado pass has become my go-to butterfly pass because it is quick and effective, allowing me to breeze through butterfly guard.

I am standing, ready to pass Henrique's seated guard.

I shoot my hands forward and latch on to Henrique's ankles.

I lift Henrique's legs off of the mat, forcing him to rock onto his back.

I maintain control of Henrique's ankles as he settles into fighting from his back. Typically, I would use one of my standing passes to set up a transition to side control, but I decide that passing from butterfly guard is the safest choice.

I press Henrique's ankles together with my hands.

Before Henrique can spread his legs, I thrust my hips forward, stuffing his feet between my legs as I drop to the mat.

7

As I kneel, I thread my arms between Henrique's knees and to the outsides of his hips. If I attempt to swim my arms around his legs, he has a much better chance of controlling my arms.

8

I press my left shoulder into Henrique's chest and press him to the mat as I slide my elbows to the outside of his hips. To prevent him from sweeping me, I lock his hooks in place by pinching my elbows to my knees, eliminating as much space as possible.

9

When I'm ready to pass Henrique's butterfly guard, I post my left hand on the inside of his right thigh.

10

Since my head is turned to the right, I begin to explode into the tornado pass by kicking my right leg into the air, following it immediately by kicking my left leg into the air, balancing on my right forearm and my forehead. If I do not elevate my hips high enough, Henrique will simply put me in his full guard, so I aim to lift my hips directly over my head.

258

While in midair, I rotate my hips to my right and push Henrique's right thigh away with my left hand.

My right knee lands first, planting against Henrique's right hip to block his attempt to re-guard me.

My left knee lands against Henrique's right shoulder. I wrap my left arm around his head and underhook his left arm with my right arm, securing side control.

LEG OVER PASS

Though the tornado pass is my first choice for passing the butterfly guard, I am sometimes forced to use a different pass if my opponent defends in the correct way. In this technique, I have successfully flattened my opponent to the mat and jumped into his butterfly guard. Before I can jump into the tornado pass, he bench presses me away, creating space. If I attempt the tornado pass in this scenario, my balance will be compromised and my opponent could counter with a sweep. When I feel that my opponent is pressing me upward, I transition to the leg-over pass to protect my base and to pass his guard.

1

I am in Henrique's butterfly guard, pinching my elbows against his hips and to my knees to keep him flat on his back.

2

Before I can set up the tornado pass, Henrique presses my chest away with both hands. With my head no longer against his chest, I know that the tornado pass is not an option.

3

I post my hands on Henrique's stomach and lift my hips by posting on my toes.

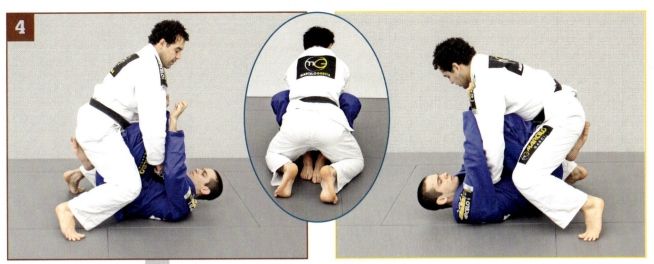

I hop onto my feet, trapping Henrique's butterfly hooks between my legs.

I posture, surfing Henrique's shins as I control his knees with my hands.

I pinch Henrique's knees together with my hands.

7

I kick my left leg forward over Henrique's head.

8

I swing my left leg over Henrique's chest, allowing my hips to slide down his thighs to his left.

9

As I slide over Henrique's legs, I swim my left arm under his right arm, securing an underhook.

mG IN ACTION

I scissor my legs, turning my chest toward the mat.

Wrapping my right arm around Henrique's head, I tuck my knees against his body and establish side control.

MG FAST FACT

Stylistically, the Deep Half Guard and X Guard have risen in popularity and the 'Leg Over Pass' is a great secondary option when your initial attempt is unsuccessful and your partner gets under you.

MGInAction.com

KNEE STUFF TO MOUNT

Transitioning to the leg swing when your opponent creates space is vital because it prevents him from sitting up into a traditional butterfly guard position, where his butterfly hooks are strongest. Though your opponent's leverage is minimal when he is on his back, he can still manipulate you with his hooks to some degree. When you stand, there is a chance that he could pull you forward and attempt to elevate your hips. If your base is in jeopardy, it is too late to use the leg swing. Instead, stuff his legs between yours and jump to mount, but you must do this before he rocks you to either side.

I am in Henrique's butterfly guard, pressing my head against his chest and caging his hips with my elbows to keep him flat on his back.

Henrique plants his hands on my chest and presses me away, creating space.

I post my hands on Henrique's ribs and jump to my feet, setting up the leg swing pass.

Before I can posture, Henrique pulls me forward with his hands and with his hooks.

Working with Henrique's energy, I cup his knees with my hands.

In one motion, I shove his legs between mine and dive forward. The window to transition to mount is small, so it is important that I commit to the technique completely.

I land on Henrique's chest, straddling his torso.

I sink my hips back and post on the mat for balance, establishing mount.

MG IN ACTION

SUBMISSIONS

No grappling system is complete without submissions. My approach to submitting from the back does not employ any unusual or unorthodox submissions, since my options from the back are somewhat limited. In other positions—side control, mount, the guard— the submission variations are almost infinite. Sadly, many grapplers railroad themselves into only attacking with a handful of the traditional submissions. The fundamental techniques are fundamental for a reason, and they should not be abandoned, but too many submission opportunities are overlooked. Those are valuable chances to win the fight, chances that should not be ignored.

Rather than review the submissions you likely already know or have seen in other books, I have collected an assortment of my favorite moves that may seem unorthodox but are still effective and useful. Many of these submissions have led me to victory in numerous tournaments, either by forcing my opponent to tap or giving me the opening to transition to another submission, a sweep, or a more dominant position. In showing you these attacks, my goal is to expand the way you think about jiu-jitsu, to help you see the possibilities of each position, simultaneously developing your arsenal and giving you the awareness to explore new techniques on your own.

CHOKES

The guillotine choke is hardly an unknown submission. The newest white belts have an instinctive familiarity with the guillotine, latching on to the neck out of desperation and straining until their arms go limp. Perhaps this is part of the reason why the guillotine has a reputation for being a "cheap" submission—too many grapplers do not know how to properly set the choke and end up squeezing their training partners' heads instead. After repeatedly failing to finish the guillotine, fighters abandon it, which creates an interesting phenomenon. Since so few people use the guillotine effectively, many fighters forget to naturally prevent the guillotine in the way that they might prevent an armbar or a triangle choke.

When I realized that the guillotine choke had the potential to be a versatile and dangerous submission, I began to experiment with setups and finishes. I did not like the idea of pulling closed guard to finish the guillotine because if I lost the guillotine I would be stuck on my back. Furthermore, I felt that the closed guard did not provide a strong enough angle for finishing the choke consistently. My solution was twofold:

-Like my approach to the rear naked choke, I do not slide my arm across the neck to set the choke; I jam it in as soon as the throat is exposed to apply instantaneous pressure.

-If I'm finishing the guillotine from the bottom, I prefer a guard variation where one of my legs hooks one of my opponent's legs

while my other foot goes over his back. This allows me to angle my hip into the mat, making it difficult for my opponent to escape and tripling the pressure that I can apply.

In the gym, my changes to the guillotine dramatically improved my success with the submission, but the true test would be against top-level competition. In the 2009 ADCC in Barcelona, Spain, I submitted three competitors in a row with the guillotine, using setups that I demonstrate in this chapter. The other chokes that I demonstrate may be chokes that you have never seen. These submissions are the result of more experimentation. I knew that my ability to choke was strong, so anytime I saw that the neck was open, I attacked. The more I looked, the more submission opportunities I found. I have included my favorite chokes in this book, but more important than the chokes, I want you to see how these attacks represent the philosophy that I have espoused throughout this book. Be aggressive and off-balance your opponent mentally by constantly pressuring him with sweeps and submission attempts. If he is always in danger, he will eventually make a crucial mistake that will win you the fight. Use the chokes in this chapter as inspiration and begin exploring other options on your own. Learning to see the possibilities, learning to create your own jiu-jitsu, is more valuable than any one technique.

You may notice, however, that none of the chokes that I demonstrate are "arm in" chokes, like arm triangles, brabos, triangles, or arm-in guillotines. I avoid arm-in chokes because I dislike the idea of having to fight one of my opponent's arms to get to his neck. With an arm inside, whether or not I finish the choke can become a matter of strength. When I attack the neck, I want to attack the neck and the neck alone. I want to be able to use my entire body against his throat, and that means having nothing in my way. I realize that this perspective may be somewhat controversial, but it is an opinion that I have forged through hours of experimentation and countless matches with a variety of opponent's. If you disagree, that is fine; I simply want you to understand why I am using certain submissions and not others.

ARMBARS AND OMOPLATAS

The armbar from mount is a basic jiu-jitsu technique, one that all grapplers learn, yet it is rarely used successfully in competition. Every grappler knows the armbar and is thus prepared to defend it, making it difficult to set up and apply. That is no reason to abandon the submission entirely. After all, you are faced with a similar situation when attacking with the rear naked choke. Instead of giving up on the armbar, refine your technique. In this chapter, I demonstrate two variations of the armbar from mount that address the main obstacle you will encounter from mount: strong posture.

The omoplata is like the guillotine. The majority of competitive grapplers are familiar with it, but few have explored its versatility. They only apply the omoplata from closed guard, but I wanted to distill the core components of the position so that I could apply it from a variety of positions. What I found was that anytime my opponent attempted an underhook, I could counter with the omoplata. As I refined the setups for the omoplata, I began to understand the implications. If I could consistently counter the underhook with the omopla-

ta, my opponents would hesitate to underhook me, making it much easier for me to control the pace of the match.

When you apply the omoplata, no matter from what position, keep the following principles in mind to maximize the effectiveness of your attack:

-When you throw your leg over to begin the omoplata, drive your foot to the mat and turn onto your side to break your opponent's posture. This is the most important part of the move. If you fail to break his posture, he can escape the submission, possibly putting you in a bad position.

-Prevent your opponent from executing a forward roll by draping one of your arms over his back.

-To apply the submission, clasp both of your hands together under his far armpit or grip the fabric of his gi on his far shoulder. Then drive your hips toward your opponent's head to finish the submission.

I have included techniques for troubleshooting common counters to the omoplata, but you should still strive to perfect the submission in its most basic form. When you combine a strong omoplata with strong countertactics, you will have mastered the submission.

THROAT CRUSH

The throat crush is a simple but often-ignored submission. Unlike a traditional guillotine, the throat crush does not require you to pass your opponent's head into your armpit. Instead, your chest keeps his head in position while a squeeze drives your forearm into his windpipe, creating a quick, painful, and effective submission. Personally, I tend to threaten the throat crush when I am trying to set up a takedown. I bait my opponent into lowering his chest so that he can better protect his legs from doubles and singles, tricking him into inadvertently exposing his neck. By hunting for the throat crush, I succeed even if the submission fails. What I mean by that is that attacking my opponent's neck from this position will make him hesitant to bend over to protect his legs, increasing the chances of my initiating and completing a shot.

Henrique and I are on our feet, looking for takedowns.

To trick Henrique into exposing his neck, I lower my hips to make him think that I am looking to shoot. He mirrors me to protect his legs.

3 I shoot my hands forward, looping my left hand to the back of Henrique's head and my right forearm under his chin.

4 I pull Henrique's head down with my left hand and set my right forearm under his chin.

5 I set my chest on the back of Henrique's head, replacing my left hand.

6

I grab my right hand with my left, leaving Henrique's head centered against my chest.

7

To finish the submission, I pinch my elbows against the side of Henrique's head and pull my arms to my chest, driving my right forearm into his throat. He is forced to tap.

THROAT CRUSH TO GUILLOTINE

When you set the throat crush, protecting your legs is difficult because both of your arms are committed to the choke. If your opponent takes you down, you will no longer be in a position to use your chest to control his head, so you must switch to a guillotine choke if you want to finish the fight. Fortunately, the throat crush provides you with enough control to make this transition relatively easy, but do it quickly to maximize the pain of the guillotine. As you work through the sequence below, pay close attention to my arm positioning when I set the finish. My variation of the guillotine may be subtle, but the details make a huge difference in the effectiveness of the choke.

I lower my hips to trick Henrique into mirroring my position. As soon as he lowers his head, I shoot my arms forward, cupping the back of his head with my left hand and jamming my right forearm under his chin to set up the throat crush.

I set my chest on the back of Henrique's head, replacing my left hand so that I can grip my right hand.

3

I fold my elbows against the sides of Henrique's head, but he counters by wrapping his arms around my legs for a takedown.

4

Henrique drives forward and takes me down. I land on my butt.

5

No longer having the proper angle to finish the throat crush, I use my throat crush to pull Henrique's head under my right armpit.

6 I fall backward toward my right shoulder, beginning to point my left elbow toward the ceiling and in front of his right shoulder. Notice that his right leg is between my legs. Which leg I choose to half guard will be an important part of the finish, and that process begins in this step.

7 I cross my ankles to trap Henrique's right leg in my half guard. To finish the choke, I angle my left elbow upward and wedge it in front of his right shoulder. I then bridge my hips to jam the blade of my wrist into his throat. By half guarding his right leg instead of his left, I trap his hips on the same side of my body as his head, which prevents him from circling away from the choke to escape.

By digging the blade of my wrist into my opponent's windpipe, I create an instantaneous, sharp pain before ever cutting off his airflow or circulation. The angle of my left elbow and the positioning of my hands allow me to better aim the blade of my wrist and also limit my opponent's ability to protect his neck by stacking through the choke.

COUNTER SINGLE-LEG TO GUILLOTINE CHOKE

When my opponent attacks with a single-leg, I always look to force his head to the outside of my leg so that I can take his back, a technique that I demonstrated earlier in the book. If my opponent's head is positioned to the inside of my leg and I cannot move it, the guillotine is my best option for countering. Many grapplers use the guillotine to counter takedowns and have mixed results. At first, my finish rate was inconsistent as well, but through a great deal of experimentation, I refined the position to the point that I am as confident in my guillotine as I am with my rear naked choke. In the previous technique, I finished the guillotine from half guard and set my elbow in front of his shoulder, pointing to the sky. In this variation, I have enough space to throw one of my legs over my opponent's back, which eliminates the need to position my arm in front of his shoulder by strengthening the angle of the choke.

Henrique has snatched my right leg and is pinching it between his knees, attempting to finish the single. I already tried to push his head to the outside of my right leg with my left hand, but he resisted.

I control the back of Henrique's head with my left hand and point the knuckles of my right hand to make it easier to slip under his chin.

I punch my right hand under Henrique's chin, maintaining a clenched fist to give him less surface area to grab if he chooses to defend.

I press downward on the back of Henrique's head with my left hand, folding his neck over my right wrist.

I set my chest on the back of Henrique's head, replacing my left hand, just like I would do to set a throat crush.

I grip my right hand with my left, using a ball and socket style grip to hide as much of my right hand as possible, making it ever harder for Henrique to protect his neck. In this step, my arms are positioned almost as though I am attacking with a throat crush, and I am squeezing my elbows against his head to limit his movement.

Without loosening the position that I established in the previous step, I sit back, dragging Henrique to the mat.

As my butt hits the mat, I yank Henrique's head under my right armpit and continue to squeeze with my arms. As I reposition his head, I twist to my right.

I lie back, positioning myself on my right hip to create a stronger choking angle and to create the space for my left leg to begin swinging up and over Henrique's back.

I lock my heel against Henrique's left hip. To finish the choke, I squeeze my arms into my chest and extend my legs to drive my forearm into his neck. I use an elbow angle similar to the previous guillotine, but because my leg is over his back, I do not need to have it in front of his shoulder.

Unlike the previous guillotine, it is not necessary for me to wedge my gripping arm in front of my opponent's shoulder to finish the choke when I can throw my leg over his back and angle my hips toward his neck. However, the positioning of my hands is still important, and I strive to achieve an arm position that is almost identical to that of the previous technique.

COUNTER SINGLE-LEG GUILLOTINE CHOKE (OPTION 2)

In most cases, I am able to initiate the guillotine choke by jamming my hand under my opponent's chin, like I did in the previous technique. If my opponent's chin is tucked, I turn away to yank my leg free of the single, but if his neck opens up, as it often will, I switch back into the guillotine right away. Once I have access to my opponent's neck, the finish itself is the same. Remaining aggressive and attacking the neck at every opportunity mentally breaks your opponent, and using little tricks like this technique to set up a choke may seem obvious in instructional form, but if you analyze one of your matches, you are likely to see at least one point that you missed where your opponent's neck was vulnerable. I had a similar realization, which is part of the reason why I began relentlessly hunting for guillotines.

Henrique is attacking my right leg with a single-leg takedown. I attempted to shove his head outside of my right leg, but he resisted, and his chin is tucked tightly, so the previous guillotine entry is unavailable.

I set my right hand on Henrique's back and press him away.

Using my right arm to prevent Henrique from driving into me, I turn away and attempt to yank my right leg out of his hands. Notice how this movement exposes his neck.

In one motion, I turn back toward Henrique, jam my right wrist under his chin, and control the back of his head with my left hand.

I stuff Henrique's head toward that mat with my left hand to fold his neck over my right wrist.

6

I set my chest on the back of Henrique's head, freeing my left hand so that I can grip my right hand.

7

I use the throat crush grip to drag Henrique to the mat as I sit backward.

8

I jerk Henrique's head under my right armpit as I rock onto my right hip and swing my left leg into the air.

MG IN ACTION

Wrapping my left leg over Henrique's back, I drive my hips forward and twist my left elbow upward to jam the blade of my wrist into his windpipe, ending the fight.

MG FAST FACT

In his early competitive career, Marcelo used the triangle as his primary submission attack. As he gained more experience as a fighter, he discovered it was a better use of his time to develop a submission game that would be equally effective against all opponents. As a result, he began to focus more on submissions where like the RNC, Guillotine, and North South, there is a higher rate of finishes against a larger and stronger opponent.

MGInAction.com

COUNTER SEATED SINGLE-LEG TO THROAT CRUSH GUILLOTINE

The throat crush is also available when I am attacking a seated opponent. Though my opponent is not standing, the mechanics of the setup and the finish are not all that different. I use his single-leg attempt to create an opening for the throat crush, and I finish the choke by controlling him with my chest and my elbows as I dig my wrist into his windpipe. The subsequent technique, the next option in this series, is like the second option in the standing series: I fake an attempt to escape the single-leg to expose my opponent's neck to the throat crush. These commonalities, this overlap in techniques, simplifies my game and creates a high level of efficiency. By hunting the same submissions in a variety of scenarios, I accumulate countless hours or practice, which makes my submissions sharp and deadly.

I am standing and am looking to pass Henrique's seated guard.

I bend over and latch on to Henrique's ankles with my hands.

I throw Henrique's legs into his chest to force him to roll onto his back.

I step my right leg forward between his legs. As Henrique sits up to regain his seated guard and to attack my right leg, I lower my right hand, aiming to hook it under his chin.

Henrique commits to the single-leg, and I guide his chin over my right hand by controlling the back of his head with my left hand. Once his head is in position, I set my chest on the back of his head and grip my right fist with my left hand.

To apply finishing pressure, I fold my elbows against the sides of Henrique's head as I pull his neck upward into my chest to drive the blade of my wrist into his throat. From this position, I can rest my elbows on my thighs to stabilize my position if I feel that I need to.

COUNTER SEATED SINGLE-LEG TO THROAT CRUSH GUILLOTINE (OPTION 2)

When I bait a seated opponent into attempting a single-leg takedown, there is always a chance that his grip on my leg will be so tight that his chin will be inaccessible. We covered a similar scenario in the standing throat crush series, and the solution here is the same as the solution there: I yank my leg away to momentarily expose my opponent's neck to the choke. The window for the choke will be small, so you must work quickly. If in the scramble your opponent's head drifts to the outside of your trapped leg, take his back using the transition that you learned earlier in the book.

Henrique is playing a seated guard, and I am standing, looking to pass or to set up a submission.

I shoot my arms to the mat and grab Henrique's ankles.

I lift Henrique's legs into the air, forcing him to rock backward.

Feeling that Henrique will not remain on his back, I step my right leg forward between his legs.

As I suspected, Henrique sits up and reaches for my right leg, which I have offered to him as an easy target.

6

Henrique wraps his arms around my right leg, attempting a single-leg. I try to jam my right wrist under his chin, but there is not enough space.

7

To create an opening for the throat crush, I pull my right knee away from Henrique's chest without moving my foot.

8

As Henrique attempts to close the space that I created in the previous step, I control the back of his head with my left hand and wedge my right wrist under his chin.

I drop my chest on the back of Henrique's head to fold his neck over the blade of my right wrist.

To end the fight, I pinch my elbows against his head and drive my right wrist upward into his neck, creating a quick, sharp pain.

CHOKES

FAILED THROAT CRUSH TO FORWARD ROLL TO BRIDGE CHOKE

If you have read the previous chapters or have read my previous book, The X-Guard, you may have noticed that—no matter what—I have my next technique planned. As much as I may want to finish a submission, I have to respect the fact that my opponent wants to win as badly as I do, and that he will exhaust every counter and escape in his arsenal before surrendering. Even a submission as quick and as brutal as the throat crush can be countered, and if I am not ready to react to my opponent's defense, he could surprise me and escape, which could be the beginning of the end for me. If I have the neck, I want to keep it, so when my opponent rolls backward to escape the throat crush or sweeps me over his shoulder, I continue to squeeze and finish the throat crush by bridging into my opponent. Even though the position is different, the principles that make the throat crush effective remain the same. As I roll over, I must keep my opponent's head against my chest. If I allow him to slip to either side, I will lose the choke.

Henrique was playing a seated guard, and I baited him into the throat crush, which I am now working to finish. He latches on to my legs, and I anticipate that he intends to sweep me.

Henrique defends the throat crush by rolling backward, pulling me with him with his hands and hooking my leg with his right foot. As I roll, I do my best to keep his head centered against my chest.

3

I land on my back, but I still have not released my choke.

4

I pull my heels close to my butt and pinch my elbows against the side of Henrique's head to tighten my position.

5

To finish the choke, I bridge into Henrique, forcing his neck into my hands as I pull them toward my chest. He has no choice but to submit.

BAIT UNDERHOOK GET-UP TO MOUNTED GUILLOTINE

The guillotine is an underused submission, and it is available from more positions than many grapplers realize. For example, I have had a great deal of success setting it up while attempting to pass my opponent's half guard. When I am working to pass, my opponent is fixated on maintaining his guard and setting up attacks of his own. He does not expect me to attack his neck. Typically, passing the guard is my priority when I am on top, but if my opponent grabs my ankle when I am standing in his half guard, he hinders my ability to use my favorite passes. By controlling my ankle, however, my opponent has one less hand protecting his neck, so I drop in to a guillotine choke. If I miss the guillotine, I will return to passing because my opponent will undoubtedly release my ankle to defend against the choke.

I am standing in Henrique's half guard, working to pass. Before I can initiate one of my favorite half guard passes, he cups my right ankle with his left hand.

Recognizing that Henrique's grip on my ankle exposes his neck to a choke, I kick my left leg into the air and swing it behind me, gripping his right knee with my left hand for balance. It is important that I initiate this movement before he establishes a De La Riva guard.

As I circle my left leg behind me, I lower my hips to the mat and begin to loop my right arm around Henrique's head.

I land on my right hip, posting my left foot behind me to keep from being rolled over. With my base established, I rest the weight of my torso on Henrique's chest and wrap his neck with my right arm, squeezing it into my armpit.

Without loosening the squeeze of my right arm, I pull my left hand to my chest, pointing my fingers toward Henrique's neck. I then latch on to my right hand with my left hand. To finish the choke, I drive the blade of my wrist upward and push off of my left foot to drive more of my weight on top of his neck, grinding my ribs into his throat and his carotid artery.

CHOKES

NORTH-SOUTH CHOKE

The north-south choke is one of my all-time favorite submissions. I used this choke twice in the 2007 ADCC, submitting Pablo Popovitch and Mario Miranda, two extremely talented and athletic competitors. Their posture was strong, but I used subtle shifts in my body weight to expose their necks to the north-south choke. I have shown that this technique will work against top-level competition, but many people struggle to finish the choke because they do not properly expose the neck or maximize the leverage of their weight to apply finishing pressure. Once you perfect the details, you will consistently finish this choke. Though I demonstrate the technique in the gi, you may have more success with this submission if you begin to practice it without the gi first. The fabric and friction of the gi can make it difficult for you to feel your opponent's positioning, which can make finding the correct angle for the choke somewhat challenging. If you master the north-south choke in no-gi, it will be much easier for you to apply it with the gi.

I am in side control. Henrique is protecting his arms by tucking his elbows and framing against my body.

I shift my chest to my right, away from my Henrique's left arm.

Pressing my chest down into Henrique's left arm, I shift back to my left, forcing his left arm away from his neck.

Without relieving the pressure on Henrique's left arm, I drape my left arm over his right arm.

I jam Henrique's right elbow to the mat with my left arm, prying his right hand away from his neck. If I am only able to move his right arm an inch with this movement, I will have enough space to set my choke.

6

With my pressure on Henrique's arms remaining constant, I loop my right arm around his head. Keeping his neck exposed by controlling his arms is important. If Henrique regains his posture, I will have to restart the technique.

7

I wrap Henrique's head with my right arm. Notice that my right forearm is parallel with his shoulder line. This angle will be ideal for the choke.

8

I flop onto my right hip, smashing my ribs into Henrique's head to force him to look away. If this pressure were absent, he could turn to face me and escape the choke.

9

I step my left leg back, circling toward the north-south position, still driving my weight into Henrique's face.

10

As I swing my right leg under my left leg to transition to the north-south position, I slide my left hand under my right, palm up, and lock my hands. By keeping my chest low in this position, I hold Henrique in place and eliminate the space that he could use to escape.

11

I sprawl my legs back and scoot my hips away from Henrique to sink my right shoulder into his neck. I look to my left and use the combination of my arm squeeze and my weight on his throat to force him to tap.

ARMBARS AND OMOPLATAS

STRAIGHT ARMBAR FROM MOUNT

The straight armbar from mount is a classic Brazilian jiu-jitsu technique that most white belts learn within their first week of training. Though it may not be an unorthodox submission like other attacks that I address in this chapter, it is overlooked in the sense that many grapplers are neglecting key details for setting and finishing the armbar, leading them to lose the submission or to completely ignore the opportunity to use it. To be successful with the straight armbar from mount, you need to recognize the appropriate time to apply the submission and how to set the armbar in such a way that it is tight and difficult for your opponent to defend. To do that, you need to completely expose one of his arms, which is to say that you must force him to give up his posture. At the lower levels, it is not uncommon for an opponent to expose his arm as he attempts to escape, but as you climb the ranks, that will happen less and less, requiring you to create the opening rather than relying on your opponent making a mistake. Use your chest to manipulate your opponent's arm, moving it out of posture. The mechanics at work here are similar to the movement that you used to set up the north-south choke. It is an incredibly useful skill to master, so put the hours into perfecting it.

I am in mount, and Henrique has tucked his elbows against his chest to establish posture.

I grab Henrique's left triceps with my right hand.

I pull Henrique's left shoulder off of the mat with my right hand, pointing his left elbow into my stomach.

I drop my chest on Henrique's left arm, blocking him from turning his back flat to the mat.

Staying low, I drive my chest forward, pushing Henrique's left arm across his chest, out of posture.

I slide my right knee up Henrique's body and position it behind his head. By moving my leg high on his body, I can hold his left arm in place with my leg and hip, freeing me to lift my chest.

As I lift my chest, I hop my left foot into Henrique's right armpit, establishing a technical mount as I begin to turn to my left.

I hook Henrique's left arm with my left arm, hugging it to my chest.

MG IN ACTION

I press down into Henrique's chest with my right hand as I lean to my left, lessening the amount of weight resting on my right leg.

With my left shoulder nearly touching Henrique's left knee, I swing my right leg over his head. With my right hand still on his chest, I block him from sitting up to escape the submission.

I set my right leg over Henrique's face and immediately pinch my knees and make my legs heavy to stabilize the position as I sit back.

To finish the armbar, I lean back, transferring my left hand to Henrique's left wrist as I fall. I use my hands to point his left thumb to the ceiling, aligning his elbow joint for the submission, and I bridge my hips to apply the finishing pressure. Notice that I favor positioning his left arm to my left. I do this to prevent the hitchhiker escape, which requires him to set his arm on my right side and point his thumb toward the mat as he circles away from me.

ARMBARS AND OMOPLATAS

OVER-THE-SHOULDER ARMBAR FROM MOUNT

Using your chest to force your opponent's arms out of posture is a high-percentage tactic for setting up a straight armbar from mount. Unfortunately, no technique is effective 100 percent of the time. If chest pressure fails, attempt to pummel inside of your opponent's arms to weaken his posture. The benefit of looking for this technique after the previous technique is that your attempt to smash his arms with your chest can make him more susceptible to the pummel. The reverse is also true, so learn to alternate between the two setups to maximize your chances of finishing the fight. If you perfect both techniques, it will be as though you are using two attacks at once, which will eventually overwhelm your opponent and force him to make a mistake.

I have mount, but Henrique is hiding his arms exceptionally well, making it difficult for me to attack with the traditional straight armbar.

I suck my right arm to my ribs and point the fingers of my right hand, slipping them under Henrique's left forearm.

3

I punch my right arm forward, shooting under Henrique's left forearm to pry it out of posture.

4

I set my right elbow on the mat and lower my chest to prevent Henrique from swimming his left arm back into posture.

5

To tighten the position, I slide my right knee to my right elbow, pinching them together to trap Henrique's left arm under my right armpit.

6

Leaning my weight onto my right knee and right elbow, I latch on to Henrique's right wrist with my left hand and press it against his chest.

7

With Henrique's right wrist pinned, I lift my left leg and swing it over his right arm.

8

I throw my left leg over Henrique's shoulder as though I were going to transition to a mounted triangle.

I lean back and to my left, centering my weight on Henrique's chest to free my right leg. It's important that I do not lean too far back or to the side, lest he roll me.

I kick my right leg forward, pinching my knee against Henrique's left elbow as I slide my butt off of his chest and on to the mat next to his hip. To finish the armbar, I squeeze my knees together and bridge my hips slightly. If his arm slips out of my armpit, I will transition to a traditional armbar finish.

OMOPLATA FROM BUTTERFLY GUARD

The omoplata is a well-known submission in Brazilian jiu-jitsu, but most fighters only think of applying it from the closed guard. My approach varies drastically from the traditional mind-set. If my opponent's arm is outstretched, searching for an underhook, I will attack with the omoplata, regardless of whether I am on top or on bottom or what kind of guard I have. In this technique, I start out attempting to use my butterfly guard to sweep my opponent. When my opponent begins to pummel his underhooks in, I throw my back to the mat to escape his control and extend at least one of his arms. Once his arm is extended, I attack with the omoplata. The approach may seem unorthodox, but I have had a great deal of success with this technique, and if you drill it and begin to look for it when you roll, you will have success with it too. Keep in mind that part of what makes this omoplata successful is its place in my butterfly guard system, which I detailed at length in my first book, The X-Guard.

Henrique is kneeling, and I am playing a seated guard.

I extend my legs and set my feet between his legs to set up a transition to butterfly guard.

Digging my heels into the mat, I scoot my butt forward and immediately work to establish an underhook and an overhook.

Henrique is faster than me. He shoots both of his arms under my armpits and drives forward to flatten me out, nullifying the leverage of my butterfly guard.

To counter Henrique, I hop my feet out from between his legs and onto his hips as I sit back.

6

Leaning to my left hip, I press Henrique's hips away with my feet to stretch him out, exposing his left arm to the omoplata.

7

I grab high on Henrique's left arm with my right hand and kick my right leg into the air.

8

With my right leg extended, I swing it over his left shoulder and slam it to the mat to dominate his posture.

9

While my right leg remains heavy, I slip my left leg out from underneath Henrique.

10

I rotate my back to the mat, shifting my right shoulder toward Henrique's hips as I cup his left elbow with my right hand.

11

Without releasing Henrique's left elbow, I throw my left arm over his back to sit up.

Once I have sat up, I grab his right shoulder with both hands to block him from somersaulting forward to escape.

I fold both of my legs under me and drive my hips toward Henrique's head to break his shoulder. If I am not wearing the gi or feel that I need more control to finish the omoplata, I proceed to the next step before maneuvering my hips for the submission.

For more control, I loop my right arm under Henrique's right arm and lock my hands together, pulling his right arm back and toward my chest. From here, the angle of my finish is the same. I drive my hips toward his head to complete the shoulder lock.

OMOPLATA ROLL TO MOUNTED ARMBAR

Even if you catch your opponent by surprise with your omoplata, the nature of the position can make the shoulder lock difficult to finish for a number of reasons. The most common problem I encounter is not being able to escape my bottom leg, which prevents me from rotating and sitting up to finish the submission. Experienced competitors know that I need the bottom leg free to execute the omoplata, so they will stall the position by dropping their weight and trapping my leg. If I do not have an answer for this common stall tactic, my opponent will have time to think and may begin to free his arm from danger. I cannot let this happen. Isolating his arm is too big of an advantage to give up. If I cannot finish the omoplata, I use the position to mount my opponent and finish the fight with an armbar. What seemed like a disadvantage for me—having my leg trapped, unable to finish the omoplata—becomes the key for getting a different submission.

Henrique is kneeling, and I am seated.

I extend my legs and set my feet between Henrique's legs.

As I scoot my butt forward to establish butterfly guard, Henrique shoots forward, establishes double underhooks, and begins to drive me onto my back.

4

As I fall back, I set my feet on Henrique's hips. I lean onto my left hip and press his hips away with my feet, stretching him out.

5

I swing my right leg out and up, beginning to attack Henrique's left shoulder with an omoplata.

6

I throw my right leg over Henrique's left shoulder, but he latches on to my left leg with his hands to prevent me from freeing my leg and finishing the omoplata.

7

With my left leg trapped, I opt to set up a sweep by setting my right shin against the left side of Henrique's head.

8

I throw my chest forward, sitting up onto my left elbow.

mς IN ACTION

9 I rotate my hips and chest toward the mat, posting on my hands and pinching my knees as I begin to force Henrique to roll forward.

10 Henrique rolls onto his back, and I continue to rotate, turning my hips toward the sky.

11 As I rotate, my butt naturally slides down Henrique's ribs to the mat. By pinching my knees throughout the sweep, I have kept his left arm trapped against my right hip.

12 I grab my right knee with my left hand.

13 To break Henrique's arm, I squeeze my knees together, pulling my right knee into his left elbow with my right hand for additional strength and torque.

SPRAWL TO OMOPLATA

I use the omoplata from butterfly guard when I am afraid of losing position because of underhooks. And that is what makes the omoplata beautifully versatile. In many positions, I can counter the underhook—which typically means that I am in danger and beginning to lose control of the fight—with a strong submission attempt. I have said time and time again that my philosophy is to always be attacking, and looking for the omoplata when my opponent begins to sink an underhook lets me do just that, even if I may be close to losing my dominant position. In this technique, my opponent is close to finishing a double-leg, despite my best attempts to sprawl. I use his commitment to the takedown to sink the omoplata as he transitions from the double-leg to top control. I can accept the fact that I have been taken down and am in a bad position, but my aggression keeps me attacking. If I am attacking, I'm winning.

Henrique and I are on our feet, fighting for grips and looking for takedowns.

Henrique changes levels and shoots in, planting his right knee on the mat as he wraps his arms around my legs.

I kick my legs back, attempting to sprawl so that I do not land on the bottom and give up two points.

MG IN ACTION

I feel that my sprawl is failing. Henrique succeeds in driving forward and sucking my legs toward his hips. When I feel that I will be taken down, I decide switch to hunting for the omoplata.

As I fall, I press Henrique's head and upper back as low as I can. At the same time, I lean onto my right hip and swing my left leg into the air.

I throw my left leg over Henrique's left shoulder as I control his right arm with my left hand. I slam my extended left leg to the right side of his head and to the mat to dominate Henrique's posture.

I slip my right leg out from underneath Henrique. If he blocks this step of the attack, I will immediately transition to the omoplata roll to set up a mounted armbar.

8 I rotate my chest to the ceiling, flex my abdominals, and extend my arms to help myself sit up.

9 As I sit up, I reach both hands to Henrique's left shoulder.

10 I grab Henrique's left shoulder with both hands and fold my legs behind me. If I feel that I need more control, I can hook my left arm underneath his left and clasp my hands together.

11 To finish the omoplata, I drive my hips toward Henrique's head. He wisely submits.

COUNTER UNDERHOOK ESCAPE TO ARMBAR FROM SIDE CONTROL

The omoplata and the armbar are closely related submissions. They are like the hook and the cross. The flow together smoothly, and they set each other up. In this technique, I am again countering an underhook with an omoplata-like movement. I could potentially finish an armbar or an omoplata from this entry, but my opponent ultimately decides his fate. If his back is mostly flat to the mat, I will sit back for the armbar. If he turns to his knees, I will transition to the omoplata. Forcing one or the other would waste valuable energy, so I have trained myself to feel my opponent's position and to make an instantaneous judgment of which submission to use. In time, you too will develop this awareness.

I have Henrique in side control.

Henrique points the fingers of his left hand and pummels his left underhook in.

Henrique commits to his escape by bridging and stretching his left arm to the ceiling. As he performs that movement, I lift my right leg and swing it over his ribs.

I plant my right foot, beginning to trap Henrique's left arm between my right thigh and right triceps.

I slide my right elbow up the outside of my right thigh to pinch Henrique's left arm into my right armpit, trapping it.

I press Henrique's face to the mat with my left hand to further expose his left arm and left shoulder.

Balancing my weight on Henrique's upper body, I thread my right foot over his head.

To begin transitioning to the armbar, I post my right hand out to my right and lean my right hip to the mat. Notice how my right triceps is still pressed tightly against Henrique's left arm even when I am posting it on the mat. This keeps his arm trapped.

As my right hip nears the mat, I swivel my hips toward the ceiling. I lean back, pinching my knees and raising my hips. I apply this submission slowly to give Henrique ample time to tap because the pressure of this arm lock is incredibly strong.

ARMBARS AND OMOPLATAS

COUNTER ARMBAR ESCAPE WITH OMOPLATA

When I counter an underhook escape with an armbar, slowing and stalling my opponent long enough to finish the arm lock can be difficult. I initiated my attack when he was part of the way through an escape, and he could continue that momentum even as I attempt to hyperextend his arm. Though a scramble could occur, I do not want the chaos to cost me my position or the fight. To protect myself, I have a backup plan ready, which is to transition into an omoplata variation if I cannot keep my opponent on his back. The setup for the armbar makes it relatively easy for me to switch to the omoplata, and the way that I finish the omoplata in this sequence is ideal for besting an opponent bent on scrambling out of your clutches.

Henrique is trapped in my side control, and he is fighting to escape.

Henrique begins to slide his left hand under my armpit.

Henrique shoots his left arm to the ceiling and bridges. To counter his escape, I post on my left hand for balance and throw my right leg over his hips.

MG IN ACTION

4

I plant my right foot on the mat before Henrique can turn to his knees.

5

I grab my right shin with my right hand and pinch my elbow to my ribs to lock Henrique's left arm in my armpit.

6

I press Henrique's face to the mat with my left hand and pass my right foot over his head.

While still trapping his left arm, I post my right hand on the mat behind Henrique and begin to lower my hips.

As I turn toward Henrique to apply the armbar finish, he kicks his legs into the air.

Slamming his legs to the mat to generate momentum, Henrique begins to sit up. To prevent him from escaping completely, I transition to the omoplata finish by extending my right leg slightly and by pointing the toes of my right foot. This motion slows him down.

I hook Henrique's right arm with my right hand.

I pull Henrique's right arm behind his back with my right arm and cup his upper arm with my left hand, controlling him with a position similar to a crucifix.

I kick my left leg upward and set my right ankle in the bend of my left knee. If I feel that I need more of an angle to finish the shoulder lock from this position, I will hip escape away from Henrique before completing this step.

To finish the omoplata, I figure-four my legs, bridge my hips, and pull on Henrique's right arm. Since he is a friend, I do this slowly so that he has time to verbally submit because he has no free hand with which to tap.

COUNTER UNDERHOOK ESCAPE TO OMOPLATA

When I am maintaining side control, having the underhook is essential. I need it to effectively control my opponent, and it makes applying submissions from the top much easier than trying to do so without the underhook. Even though my opponent is on the bottom, if he can establish the underhook, he can escape and possibly reverse the position. When I lose the battle for the underhook, I can counter with an armbar, which I demonstrated in the previous technique, but that assumes that I catch my opponent before he turns to his knees. If my opponent is strong enough and fast enough to turn to his knees, the armbar is no longer an option, but the same movement that gave me the armbar can also give me the omoplata, making it a very versatile technique.

I am in the side control position, pinning Henrique. However, he begins to snake his left arm under my right armpit.

Henrique shoots his left arm into an underhook and bridges into me to begin escaping.

Before Henrique can escape his hips, I throw my right leg over his body, posting on my hands for balance and stability.

I plant my right foot on the left side of Henrique's body and begin to trap his left arm between my right thigh and right triceps. My first thought is to attack with the armbar, but I recognize that he is now on his knees, which means that the armbar is no longer available.

To attack with the omoplata, I throw my right leg over Henrique's left shoulder as I sink my butt to the mat.

I slam my right leg to the mat to dominate Henrique's posture.

With my right leg still heavy against Henrique's left shoulder, I reach both hands to his right shoulder and latch on to his gi.

I fold my legs behind me and pull my hips toward Henrique's head to end the fight.

me IN ACTION

BUTT-SCOOT GRIP BREAK

I see many grapplers get to the omoplata position, but they struggle to finish the submission. When they encounter the slightest bit of resistance, they abandon the omoplata entirely. This is not because they lack skill or technique. They just are not thinking in the right way. If you cannot finish the omoplata, do not give up on the technique. Think of the omoplata in the same way that you think of the triangle. If you get close to the triangle position—trapping your opponent's head and one of his arms—you do not abandon the technique. You work through his defenses, step by step, breaking his posture down, securing his trapped arm, and cinching your legs tighter. Approach finishing the omoplata with the same determination. One of the most common defenses you will encounter for the omoplata is relatively simple: your opponent will grip his hands together or grab his own belt to prevent you from cranking his shoulder. To break that grip, scoot your hips away. His grip will not be able to resist the strength of your whole body.

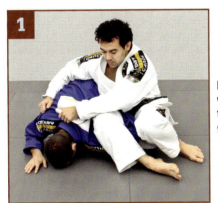

I am attacking Henrique's left arm with an omoplata, but he is defending by locking his hands together or by grabbing his belt.

To begin breaking Henrique's grip, I open my legs, posting my left foot out on the mat beside me. Notice that my hands are still gripping his gi. They will remain in that position throughout the technique.

3

Digging my feet into the mat, I scoot my hips to my left and forward, putting tension on Henrique's grip.

4

I scoot again, pulling Henrique onto his side and breaking his grip.

5

With his grip broken, I fold my legs back under me.

6

I drive my hips toward Henrique's head to finish the shoulder lock.

COUNTER FORWARD ROLL DEFENSE TO FORWARD ROLL FINISH

As with any submission, your opponent can attempt to escape at a variety of points in the omoplata. The butt-scoot break addresses one of the common defenses for the omoplata, but it assumes that I am already sitting up, ready to torque my opponent's shoulder until he taps. Most grapplers are familiar enough with the omoplata that they sense they are in danger when my leg begins to isolate one of their shoulders. Rather than resisting the movement, they use the momentum of my attack to roll forward, relieving the tension on their shoulder and escaping the submission. In the previous technique, I mentioned that you should not give up on the omoplata just because your opponent resists. When your opponent executes a forward roll to escape the omoplata, counter his roll with a forward roll of your own and use the variation of the omoplata that you learned previously as a counter for your opponent's armbar escape.

I am on the verge of finishing Henrique with an omoplata. I have his left arm isolated, and I am preparing to sit up. It's important to note that my left hand is cupping his left elbow. I need control of his left elbow for this technique to work.

As I sit up, Henrique begins to roll forward to escape the omoplata.

As Henrique rolls, I grip his left triceps with both hands and pull his left arm deep against my hip. I cannot allow his elbow to slip between my legs.

4

Henrique lands on his back and cannot free his left arm because my control is tight.

5

I fold my legs back and lean my right shoulder toward the mat.

6

I begin my forward roll by looking away from my right shoulder and driving my right shoulder toward the mat on his left side.

7

I roll forward, still controlling Henrique's left arm with both of my hands.

8

The momentum of my roll forces Henrique to sit up.

9

Rather than allow Henrique to roll out of my omoplata again, I decide to set a different finish by hooking his right arm with my right hand.

10 I pull Henrique's right arm behind his back with my right hand and grab his right triceps with my left hand as I figure-four my legs.

11 I finish the omoplata by pulling on Henrique's right arm with both of my arms and by driving my legs away, forcing his left wrist to bend toward the back of his head.

COUNTER BRIDGE ESCAPE TO OMOPLATA FINISH

Countering my opponent's forward roll with a forward roll of my own is my first option for pursuing the omoplata, but if my opponent is truly committed to escaping the omoplata, he won't simply roll out of it and lie on his back, waiting for me to make the next move. A quality competitor will not stop trying to escape until he has freed his arm from my clutches. If I still have his arm trapped after his forward roll, he will bridge to create space to yank his arm to the mat. If I block that attempt, he is likely to use his bridge to roll me over, which is a legitimately effective escape option for him. Rolling me over could potentially put him on top and out of danger. I cannot let that happen. When my opponent bridges to escape the omoplata before I can counter his forward roll with my own forward roll, I have to first prevent him from pulling his arm out of danger, and then I have to position myself in such a way that his bridge and roll actually puts him back into the omoplata.

Henrique just used a forward roll to escape my omoplata. He is now on his back, and I am preparing to use a forward roll to counter his escape by cupping his left elbow with both hands and pulling it against my right thigh.

Before I can execute a forward roll, Henrique bridges, blocking my ability to somersault and setting himself up to transition to his knees to free his arm.

Henrique begins to turn over his right shoulder. I lean in that direction and post my right hand on the mat to keep myself above and ahead of him.

As Henrique turns to his knees, I maintain a tight grip on his left arm with my left hand and allow him to rotate underneath me, which puts him right back into the omoplata.

Henrique successfully transitions to his knees but has returned to the start of an omoplata finish.

Before Henrique can roll out again, I drape my right arm over his back to control his hips.

Confident that I am in complete control, I grab Henrique's right shoulder with both hands, fold my legs behind me, and drive my hips toward his head to finish the fight.